Know Your
Pfaff Hobbylock

Other books available from Chilton:

Robbie Fanning, Series Editor

Contemporary Quilting Series

Fast Patch: A Treasury of Strip-Quilt Projects, by Anita Hallock

Fourteen Easy Baby Quilts, by Margaret Dittman

Machine-Quilted Jackets, Vests, and Coats, by Nancy Moore

Putting on the Glitz, by Anne Boyce and Sandra L. Hatch

The Quilter's Guide to Rotary Cutting, by Donna Poster

Scrap Quilts Using Fast Patch by Anita Hallock

Speed-Cut Quilts, by Donna Poster

Creative Machine Arts Series

The Button Lover's Book, by Marilyn Green

Claire Shaeffer's Fabric Sewing Guide

The Complete Book of Machine Embroidery, by Robbie and Tony Fanning

Creative Nurseries Illustrated, by Debra Terry and Juli Plooster

Creative Serging Illustrated, by Pati Palmer, Gail Brown, and Sue Green

Distinctive Serger Gifts and Crafts, by Naomi Baker and Tammy Young

The Expectant Mother's Wardrobe Planner, by Rebecca Dumlao

The Fabric Lover's Scrapbook, by Margaret Dittman

Friendship Quilts by Hand and Machine, by Carolyn Vosburg Hall

Innovative Sewing, by Gail Brown and Tammy Young

Innovative Serging, by Gail Brown and Tammy Young

Owner's Guide to Sewing Machines, Sergers, and Knitting Machines, by Gale Grigg Hazen

Petite Pizzazz, by Barb Griffin

Sew, Serge, Press, by Jan Saunders

Sewing and Collecting Vintage Fashions, by Eileen MacIntosh

Simply Serge Any Fabric, by Naomi Baker and Tammy Young

Twenty Easy Machine-Made Rugs, by Jackie Dodson

Know Your Sewing Machine Series, by Jackie Dodson

Know Your Bernina, second edition

Know Your Brother, with Jane Warnick

Know Your Elna, with Carol Ahles

Know Your New Home, with Judi Cull and Vicki Lyn Hastings

Know Your Pfaff, with Audrey Griese

Know Your Sewing Machine

Know Your Singer

Know Your Viking, with Jan Saunders

Know Your Serger Series, by Tammy Young and Naomi Baker

Know Your baby lock

Know Your White Superlock

Teach Yourself to Sew Better Series, by Jan Saunders

A Step-by-Step Guide to Your Bernina

A Step-by-Step Guide to Your New Home

A Step-by-Step Guide to Your Sewing Machine

A Step-by-Step Guide to Your Viking

Know Your Pfaff Hobbylock

by Naomi Baker and Tammy Young

Chilton Book Company

Radnor, Pennsylvania

Published in Radnor, Pennsylvania
19089, by Chilton Book Company

Cover Design by Tony Jacobson
Designed by Martha Vercoutere
Color Photographs by Lee Phillips
Illustrations by Chris Hansen

Manufactured in the United States of
America

Library of Congress Cataloging in
Publication Data

Baker, Naomi
    Know your Pfaff Hobbylock /
    Naomi Baker and Tammy Young.

    p. cm.—(Creative machine arts
    series)
    Includes index.
    1. Serging 2. Sewing
    I. Young, Tammy. II. Title.
    III. Series.
TT713.B33245 1991   91-53045
646.2'044—dc20   CIP
ISBN 0-8019-8192-1 (hc)
ISBN 0-8019-8191-3 (pb)

2 3 4 5 6 7 8 9 0 0 9 8 7 6 5 4 3 2

Contents

Preface viii
Foreword
     by Robbie Fanning ix
Acknowledgments x
1. *Hobbylock* Basics 1
  Bonding with Your Serger
  Serging and Sewing Strategies
  How to Use This Book
  Hobbylock Features
  Hobbylock Stitch Formation
  Hobbylock Feet and Accessories
  Loving Care
2. **Ornamental
   Serging Basics** 16
  Tension—The Key to Success
    Practicing Tension Adjustment
    Balancing the Tension
  Decorative Threads
    Serging Decorative Threads
    Special Threading Tips
    Combining Thread Types
    Pressing over Decorative Thread
  Threads Other Than Decorative
  Shaping Materials
  Other Important Serging Supplies
  Ornamental Serging Sample Book
  Exploring Your Machine's
    Creative Limits
3. **Decorative Seams** 32
  Lesson 1. Basic Seams 33
    Basic Decorative Seam
    Hidden Lapped Serging
      Technique
    Reversed Decorative Seam
    Lapped Seam
    Decorative French Seam
    Mock Flat-felled Seam
    Project: Double-Bow Pillow

  **Lesson 2. Serge-bound
     Seams** 38
    Serged Seam Binding
    Serged French Binding
    Double-bound Seam
    Double-piped Seam
    Project: Hobo Bag
  **Lesson 3. Flatlocked
     Seams** 44
    Perfecting Flatlocking
    Reinforced Flatlock Seaming
    Project: Quick Slip
4. **Decorative Edges** 48
  **Lesson 4. Balanced
     Decorative Edges** 49
    Serge-scalloped Edge
    Serge-corded Edge
    Serge-corded Variations
    Picot-braid Edge
    Project: Sunburst T-shirt
  Lesson 5. Rolled Edges 54
    Lettucing
    Double Rolled Edge
    Scalloped Rolled Edge
    Serge-a-Fold
    Picot Rolled Edge
    Tuck-and-Roll
    Project: Christmas Tree Bags
  Lesson 6. Fishline Ruffles ..61
    Project: Ruffled Doily
  **Lesson 7. Wire-shaped
     Edges** 63
    Project: Wind Twister
  **Lesson 8. Reversible-edge
     Binding Stitch** 66
    Project: Wool Lap Robe
  **Lesson 9. Reversible Needle-
     wrap Stitch** 67
    Project: Quick Potholder

5. Decorative Trims, Braids, and Bindings **70**
  Lesson 10. Serged-fold Self-Braid **70**
    Project: Lace-edged Handkerchief
  Lesson 11. Quick-fused Self-Braid **73**
    Project: Quickie Shoe Bags
  Lesson 12. Serged Self-Binding **75**
    Project: Canvas Tote Bag
  Lesson 13. Double-bound Edge **78**
    Project: Show-off Pillow
  Lesson 14. Serged Piping ... **80**
    Elasticized Piping
    Mock Piping
    Elasticized Mock Piping
    Project: Serge-piped Book Cover
  Lesson 15. Serged Binding **86**
    Project: Serge-bound Table Runner
  Lesson 16. Serge-piped Binding **89**
    Project: Padded Picture Frame
  Lesson 17. Double Rolled-edge Braid and Binding **93**
    Double Rolled-edge Braid
    Double Rolled-edge Binding
    Project: Tooth Fairy Pillow
  Lesson 18. Elasticized Trims and Binding **96**
    Elasticized Trims
      Single-stretch Trim
      Double-stretch Trim
      Stretch-Trim Variations
      Braided Trim
    Elasticized Binding
    Project: Ruffled Jar Cover

  Lesson 19. Tear-away Braid **101**
    Project: Pretty Pencil Cup
  Lesson 20. Puffed Serged Braid **103**
    Project: Frog Closures
  Lesson 21. Serged Picot Braid **106**
    Single-picot Braid
    Double-picot Braid
    Picot-braid Variations
    Stretch Picot Braid
    Project: Picot-trimmed Hat
  Lesson 22. Serged Couching Braid **109**
    Project: Monogrammed Hand Towel

6. Special Decorative Serging Techniques **111**
  Lesson 23. Gathering and Shirring **111**
    Tension Gathering
    Differential-Feed Gathering
    Filler-Cord Gathering
    Thread-Chain Gathering
    Serge-shirring
    Double Chainstitch Shirring
    Project: Shirred Ponytail Tube
  Lesson 24. Serger Lace **116**
    Stabilized Lace
    Serger Lace Tucks
    Lacy Fishline Ruffles
    Lace-trimmed Wires
    Project: Serger-Lace Flower
  Lesson 25. Decorative Flatlocking **120**
    Corded Flatlocking
    Safety-Stitch Flatlocking
    Balanced Flatlocking
    Mock Hemstitching
    Serge-fagoting
    Project: Sampler Pin Cushion

Lesson 26. **Fringing** 124
Flatlocked Fringe
Tucked Fringe
Project: Fringed Triangle Scarf

Lesson 27. **Serging over Trim** 127
Flatlocking over Ribbon
Flatlocking over Lace and Ribbon
Flatlocking over Yarn
Project: Heart-shaped Jewelry Holder

Lesson 28. **Sequin, Bead, and Pearl Application** 130
Applying Beads and Pearls
Beaded Piping
Applying Sequins
Project: Bead-edged Flower

Lesson 29. **Serge-Couching** 133
Project: Couched Tree Ornament

7. **Decorative Serged Closures** 136
Lesson 30. **Lapped and Top-stitched Zippers** 136
Basic Lapped and Top-stitched Zipper
Lapped and Top-stitched Placket
Reversed Decorative Seam Zipper
Embellished Zipper Tape
Project: Serged Pencil Case

Lesson 31. **Zipped Double-bound Edge** 141
Project: Dressed-up Cosmetic Bag

Lesson 32. **Serge-picked Zippers** 144
Centered Application
Lapped Application
Project: Tailored Garment Bag

Lesson 33. **Serge-bound Buttonholes** 149
Project: Three-Button Belt

Lesson 34. **Serged Elastic Button Loops** 152
Project: Serge-finished Collar

8. **Expanding Your Artistic Possibilities** 155
Lesson 35. **Serger Chain Art** 155
Thread-Chain Cording
Thread-Chain Fringe
Thread-Chain Tassels
Project: Double-wrapped Tassel

Lesson 36. **Serged Appliqué** 161
Project: Appliquéd Evening Bag

Lesson 37. **Serger Cutwork** 165
Project: Cutwork Tablecloth

Lesson 38. **Embellished Fabric** 168
Constructing Fabric
Ornamenting Fabric
Project: Embellished Chiffon Scarf

Pfaff *Hobbylock* History 172
Glossary of Serging Terms 172
Mail-Order Resources 175
Other Publications by the Authors 178
Index 179

Preface

A little over a decade ago, sergers (or as they're sometimes called, overlock machines) appeared on the home-sewing market. Most sergers at that time were industrial models—big, noisy, difficult to operate, with dangerous knives, and always breaking down.

But home-sewing serger models were a very different piece of equipment than their industrial cousins. They've been domesticated, with practically all the advantages and few of the drawbacks.

Small, clean, quiet, and safe, sergers now give us creative possibilities that previously were not available to the home-sewer. During the last decade, enthusiasts have taken serger sewing from a few basic stitches and techniques to a wide variety of decorative applications and innovative uses. We call the latest developments in decorative serger sewing **ornamental serging.**

As the publisher and consulting editor of the *Serger Update* newsletter and co-authors of four previous serging books published by Chilton Book Company, we have been in a unique position to witness firsthand the exciting developments in the art of serger sewing. New equipment, technology, and notions have opened up more and more possibilities for creativity.

The Pfaff company has continued to upgrade its Hobbylock serger line so that it offers all of the latest features needed for every ornamental serging technique. Pfaff's quality engineering helps make decorative techniques easy to master.

Know Your Pfaff Hobbylock is meant to encourage you to join in this exciting trend, taking you beyond the basics and encouraging you to explore uses for the serger as an artistic instrument. We will outline methods for seaming, edge finishing, binding and trimming, and other decorative serging techniques. Simple projects are included at the end of every lesson to demonstrate skills. These projects are excellent for quick gifts, as well as for hands-on teaching.

We hope this book will encourage you to join the world of ornamental serging. Your handy *Hobbylock* will execute the basics beautifully. But taken one step further, it can easily make all of your serging projects one-of-a-kind creations.

So breeze through the basics (if you haven't already), and begin to look at all the creative serging options.

Happy ornamental serging,

Naomi Baker and Tammy Young

Foreword

Those of us lucky enough to own a serger need no convincing that as an invention, it ranks right up there with Post-it Notes, rotary cutters, and the microwave.

Yet those of us brave enough to tell the whole truth will confess that we've barely scratched the surface of our serger's capabilities.

I'm no different. Though I'm devoted to my serger, I've used it primarily to clean finish seam allowances. I'd like to do more, but my time for experimenting is limited. What I need is a master teacher at my side, coaxing me to twirl those knobs, change that thread, try this technique.

Shazam! Not one, but two master teachers have appeared through a puff of smoke. Tammy and Naomi, in the pages of this book, are exactly what you and I need. They walk us through the basics, and then lesson by lesson, teach a new technique, ending with a sample project using that technique. Some of my favorite ornamental serging techniques are the serged frog closure, elastic button loops, and double-bound seams.

For a busy sewer, this lesson format is ideal. You can try a lesson in an evening, make a sample for your notebook, then choose your favorite techniques to embellish a garment on the weekend.

By the time you finish, you will truly know your serger.

Robbie Fanning
Series Editor

Are you interested in a quarterly newsletter about creative uses of the sewing machine, serger, and knitting machine? Write to The Creative Machine-hl, PO Box 2634, Menlo Park, CA 94026.

Acknowledgments

This book would not have been possible without the full cooperation and assistance of the Pfaff American Sales Corp., manufacturer of *Hobby-lock* sergers. Special thanks to Elvi Tarien, Louise Gerigk, and the entire company management team for their enthusiastic support.

Thank you also to our professional *Serger Update* writers and other industry professionals who have pioneered serger sewing and inspired us.

We also want to thank the talented people who have helped us immeasurably in producing this book: Chris Hansen, illustration; Lee Phillips, photography; and Martha Vercoutere, book design.

Finally, many thanks go to our editor, Robbie Fanning, and our publisher's representative, Kathryn Conover, for believing in our efforts and encouraging us to write a series of brand-specific books on ornamental serging techniques.

The following are registered trademark names used in this book: *Candlelight, Decor 6, Fabric Mender Magic, Fray Check, Lycra, OK to Wash-It, Mez Alcazar, Perfect Pleater, Ripstop, Seams Great, Solvy, Stiffy, Superlock, TAC Spray Stiff, Teflon, Thinsulate, Ultrasuede, Velcro, Wash-Away,* and *Wonder-Under.*

1. Hobbylock *Basics*

- **Bonding with Your Serger**
- **Serging and Sewing Strategies**
- **How to Use This Book**
- ***Hobbylock* Features**
- ***Hobbylock* Stitch Formation**
- ***Hobbylock* Feet and Accessories**
- **Loving Care**

Bonding with Your Serger

The biggest hurdle to overcome in the exciting adventure of serger sewing is **taking the machine out of the box.** Yes, that's right! Over the years, we've found that for many home-sewers, the serger looked wonderful when demonstrated in the store. It was capable of speedy seaming, pretty rolled edges, and all sorts of decorative techniques. But when the home-sewer brought it home, the serger seemed daunting and complicated. (After all, it's an entirely different kind of machine than the sewing machine we all have known.) So into the closet it goes, just waiting for that rainy day when there's plenty of time to figure out how to use it and to practice all of those wonderful serger techniques.

Of course, the longer the serger stays in the closet, the more complex and intimidating it seems. Meanwhile, your "friendly" sewing machine is right there to fall back on.

The next hurdle in serger use occurs when we do take the machine out of the box, and the dealer has adjusted it for a perfectly balanced seam. We can serge beautifully balanced seams and edges, but heaven forbid that we might have to switch to a rolled edge or a flatlock. Horrors! That can involve taking out a needle, changing a foot and plate, and adjusting the tension settings. The thought of tackling all these separate steps seems overwhelming at first.

But just stop and consider how many different adjustments you make effortlessly on your sewing machine— winding the bobbin, threading, changing needles and feet, making stitch-length adjustments, and converting to special stitches. The serger only seems complicated at first, when we're getting used to it and to its unique method of sewing.

There's a simple answer. Take your serger out of the box, read the owner's instruction manual, and practice the various kinds of stitches available on your model. In other words, *use your serger and you'll become comfortable with it sooner than you think.*

Serger expert Sue Green-Baker calls this process "bonding." Although the term is most often used for parents' feeling toward their child or for other personal relationships, it applies nicely to serger sewing as well. As you spend more time with your machine and get to know it, you will learn its idiosyncrasies, talents, and personality. At varying times this bonding process can be frustrating, exciting, intimidating, or rewarding—and just plain fun. Sharpening your spirit of adventure can be a big help.

If serging classes are available to you, by all means take advantage of them. They're a great way to speed up the learning process, pick up tips and techniques, and have a good time in the process.

In this book, we assume that you have already learned the basics of serger sewing. Check the following list to be sure.

___ Threading
___ Changing and balancing tension
___ Changing stitch width and length
___ Adjusting for a rolled edge (Practice until you can do it effortlessly.)
___ Adjusting for flatlocking
___ Using the differential feed
___ Changing needles
___ Cleaning your machine— and oiling it
___ Clearing the stitch finger
___ Serging inside and outside corners
___ Ripping out stitches

Your instruction manual is a must. If you don't have one, buy or order one from your dealer. The manual contains detailed instructions on the basics listed above. Work your way through the manual early in your bonding process.

In addition to your manual, extensive information is available to lead you through all the machine basics and construction techniques and beyond. (Several excellent resources are listed under Other Publications by the Authors.) For all current *Hobby-lock* models, an owner's workbook and instructional video are also available.

When sergers were first introduced in the United States, their use was limited to simple seams and edge finishes. Since then, serger sewing enthusiasts have developed a great deal of exciting new information. As you get to know your serger and put it to work, you will discover a whole new world of ornamental serging possibilities.

Serging and Sewing Strategies

Your serger is a natural companion to your sewing machine. Rather than working in competition with each other, these two machines team up to offer us endless possibilities. Once you are familiar with your serger and all its potential uses, you will soon know when to use your sewing machine and when to use your serger for any project or parts of a project.

The serger is fast, finishes edges beautifully, makes neat, sturdy seams, and replicates many of the looks found in today's couture and ready-to-wear. It efficiently sews many specialty fabrics we would have hesitated to tackle in the past, including sheers, silkies, and loosely wovens. The built-in stretch of a serger stitch also makes serging a favored option for interlocks, *Lycra* blends, and sweatering.

We've often heard that the serger speeds up sewing, that it trims, seams, and overlocks in one step, that it makes beautiful rolled edges and has many decorative uses. But the one thing we don't always hear is that **serger sewing is all about edges.**

Because the loopers must go above and below the fabric in order to form an overlock stitch, most serging must necessarily be done on edges or folds. (Fig. 1-1) The one exception is a double chainstitch formed by the needle and a looper (available on the 797 model only).

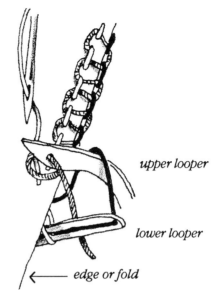

upper looper

lower looper

← edge or fold

Fig. 1-1: *Because of a serger's looper mechanism, always place serging on an edge or fold.*

The serger's ability to sew on edges includes seams (see Chapter 3), flatlocking (in Lessons 3 and 25), and edge finishing (discussed in Chapter 4). Beyond these basics, interesting variations abound.

The sewing machine, unlike the serger, has the ability to sew anywhere on a piece of fabric, not just on an edge or fold. Its straight-stitch capability—for top-stitching and edge-stitching—is essential to supplement many serger techniques. Also, its decorative stitches can be combined with serging to enhance your creativity.

Plan each of your sewing projects (whether garments, accessories, or home decorating items) in advance. Where can you add ornamental details for the most artistic and pleasing results? Consider possibilities for seams and edges. Consider decorative flatlocking. What are your other options? (Fig. 1-2)

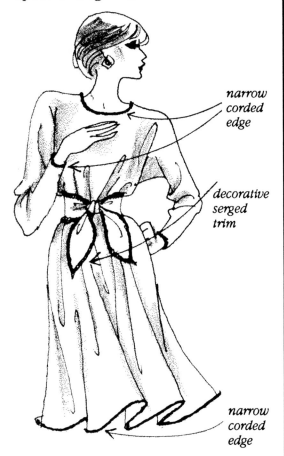

narrow corded edge

decorative serged trim

narrow corded edge

Fig. 1-2: *Plan your serging projects with decorative detail in mind.*

Experiment, then give it your best shot. But remember, subtlety can often be more pleasing than overdoing it, so you needn't decorate every edge or seam on any one project. Choose those areas where your ornamental serging will be the most effective.

The lessons and projects throughout this book are just a beginning. Once you understand the basics of serger sewing, you too can become a serger artist. It's simply a matter of focus and awareness. Ornamental serging can be applied to even the simplest T-shirt to make it look like designer sportswear (see page 53).

Practice, experimentation, failure, and success are all part of the process. So accept the challenge and join us in the latest phase of serger sewing—ornamental serging.

How to Use This Book

Know Your Pfaff Hobbylock has been designed to lead you quickly through the basics (Chapters 1 and 2) and into the fun world of ornamental serging. You'll find 38 lessons, grouped into chapters on seams; edges; trims, braids, and bindings; special techniques; serged closures; and artistic possibilities.

The lessons begin with decorative basics and progress to those requiring more advanced skill. A simple project is included at the end of every lesson so you can easily practice the techniques you have learned.

Less experienced serger users may want to follow the lessons numerically to learn basic skills before moving on to advanced ones. If you come to a term you don't understand, refer to the Glossary of Serging Terms. Experienced seamsters can easily skip around in the book, choosing to study a lesson when it applies to a current project.

Regardless of your level of experience, the Table of Contents can help you decide quickly which decorative seams, edges, bindings, or other techniques to use for a particular serger project. Once you've mastered all of the lessons in *Know Your Pfaff Hobbylock,* you'll feel comfortable selecting even the most advanced ornamental serging applications.

Hobbylock Features

The *Hobbylock* is well designed for ornamental serging. All current models have a two-step electronic foot control with both half-speed and full-speed positions. The slower half-speed setting allows greater control in ornamental serging, especially when using heavier decorative thread. Top-of-the-line models feature wide stitching (up to 9mm on the 797), excellent for many decorative applications. Current models are also designed to prevent thread from escaping out of the tension discs while serging and to use standard household needles for convenient replacement.

Hobbylock Stitch Formation

Every model of serger has one or more varying stitch options. Refer to the chart on page 6 or to your manual to determine the stitches available on

your model. If this book is your own, use a highlighter pen to mark your machine's features.

5-Thread Safety Stitch
(Fig. 1-3)

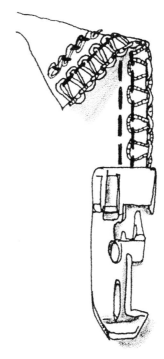

Fig. 1-3: *Stitch formation—5-thread safety stitch.*

■ Combination of a double chainstitch (on the seamline) and a 3-thread overlock stitch (on the edge).

■ Stitch width up to 9mm wide.

■ Can be converted to a double chainstitch only, a 3-thread overlock only, or a 3/4-thread overlock only.

■ The most durable and stable seam and finish, used most often on loosely wovens and for stabilizing stretchy areas.

Pfaff *Hobbylock* Features

	797	786	784	783
5-thread safety	Yes	N/A	N/A	N/A
3/4-thread overlock	Yes	Yes	Yes	N/A
3-thread overlock	Yes	Yes	Yes	Yes
2-thread double chainstitch	Yes	N/A	N/A	N/A
Number of needles	2 (3 positions)	2	2	1
Needle type	130/705H	130/705H	130/705H	130/705H
Stitch-width capacity	2.5 – 9mm	2.5 – 7.5mm	2.5 – 7.5mm	2.5 – 5.5mm
Stitch-width adjustment	Dial	Dial	Dial	Dial
Stitch-length capacity	.75 – 4mm	.75 – 4mm	.75 – 5mm	.75 – 5mm
Stitch-length adjustment	press lever/ turn handwheel	Dial	Dial	Dial
Rolled-edge adjustment	change foot	change foot	change foot	change foot
Differential feed	Yes	Yes	N/A	N/A
Snap-on presser feet	Yes	Yes	Yes	Yes

Pfaff *Hobbylock* Features

	797	**786**	**784**	**783**
Tension type	Drop-in discs	Drop-in discs	Drop-in discs	Drop-in discs
Built-in thread cutter	Yes	N/A	N/A	N/A
Accessory storage	Yes	Yes	Yes	Yes
Built-in light	Yes	Yes	Yes	Yes
Maximun sewing speed	1300 spm	1300 spm	1300 spm	1300 spm
Knife disengages	Yes	Yes	Yes	Yes
Optional blindhem foot	Yes	Yes	Yes	Yes
Optional beading foot	Yes	Yes	Yes	Yes
Optional ribbon foot	Yes	Yes	Yes	Yes
Optional elastic foot	Yes	Yes	Yes	Yes
Owner's workbook	Yes	Yes	Yes	Yes
Instructional video	Yes	Yes	Yes	Yes

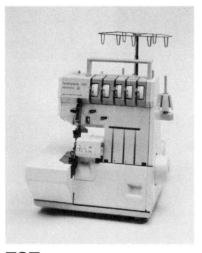

797

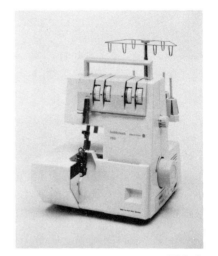

786

A Pfaff Hobbylock
Photo Gallery

784

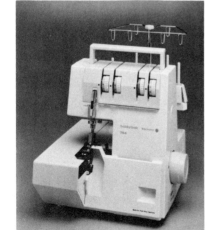

783

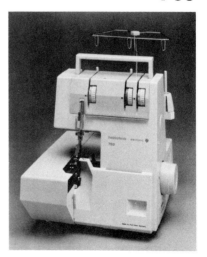

3/4-Thread Overlock Stitch

(Fig. 1-4)

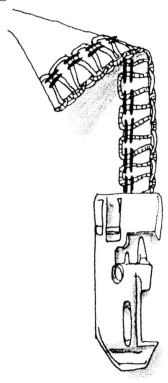

Fig. 1-4: *Stitch formation—3/4-thread overlock stitch.*

- The upper looper interlocks with the left needle, so all four threads interlock.

- Durable for seaming and decorative finishing (up to 7.5mm wide) and fully stretchable.

- Converts to a 3-thread overlock stitch by removing either needle. Use the left needle for a wide stitch and the right needle for a narrower stitch.

3-Thread Overlock Stitch

(Fig. 1-5)

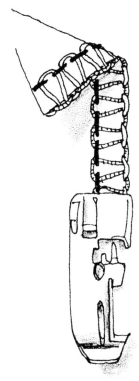

Fig. 1-5: *Stitch formation—3-thread overlock stitch.*

- Threads interlock at the seamline to form a stretchable, yet durable, seam or edge finish.

- Available on all *Hobbylock* models.

- Less bulky than a 4- or 5-thread stitch.

2-Thread Double Chainstitch

(Fig. 1-6)

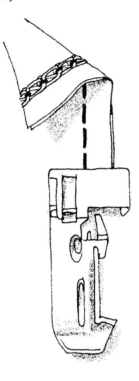

Fig. 1-6: *Stitch formation—2-thread double chainstitch.*

■ The left needle forms a straight stitch on top of the fabric, and a looper thread interlocks to form a chain on the underside (available on the 797 model only).

■ A secure stitch with little or no stretch.

■ Used for top-stitching, seaming, or hemming. When top-stitching or hemming from the underside (with the chain on the right side), a more pronounced stitching line is visible.

Hobbylock Feet and Accessories

All *Hobbylock* models have special feet and accessories to make ornamental serging easier. Both standard and optional presser feet have a snap-on feature that allows for ease in changing from one foot to another as well as unrestricted access when threading and changing needles. (Fig. 1-7) (Feet for the 780 series machines are not interchangeable with the 790 feet.)

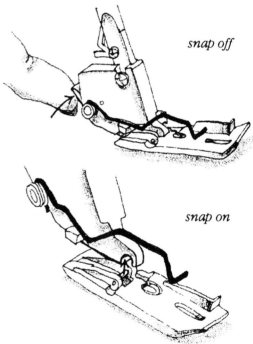

snap off

snap on

Fig. 1-7: *Snap-on feature allows presser feet to be removed quickly for switching to optional feet or for easier threading and needle changing.*

Narrow rolled-edge foot (Fig. 1-8)—To serge a narrow rolled edge, you will need to change to a rolled-edge presser foot which comes as a standard accessory with all *Hobbylock* models. (See Lesson 5 for detailed rolled-edge instructions.)

797

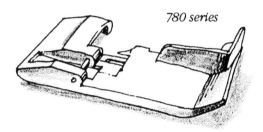

780 series

Fig. 1-8: *The rolled-edge foot is a standard* Hobbylock *accessory.*

Blindhem foot (Fig. 1-9)—This handy optional foot is available for all *Hobbylock* models. In addition to blindhemming (instructions are included with the foot), it is ideal for serged tucks and for accurately guiding serger stitching along a fold. For specific uses, see perfecting flatlocking (Lessons 3 and 25) and serger lace (Lesson 24).

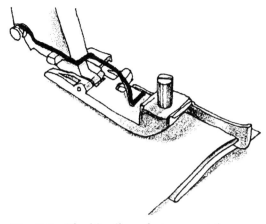

Fig. 1-9: *The blindhem foot accurately guides stitching along an edge or fold.*

Elastic foot (Fig. 1-10)—An elastic foot is available as an optional accessory on all *Hobbylock* models. It easily guides and stretches 3/8"- and 1/2"-wide elastic during application. (Narrower width elastic can also be applied with the elastic foot, but it may be difficult to guide accurately.) The amount of tension can be adjusted using a tension-control screw to alter the amount of stretch. See elasticized trims (Lesson 18) and serge-shirring (Lesson 23) for applications.

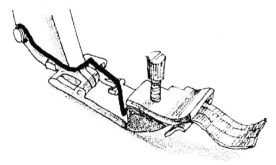

Fig. 1-10: *The elastic foot guides elastic and controls the stretch.*

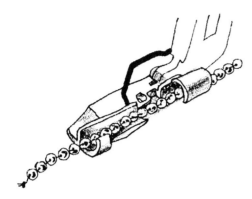

Fig. 1-11: *The beading foot guides trim accurately between the needle and the knife.*

Beading foot (Fig. 1-11)—Pearls and beads can be easily attached using a beading foot, available for all *Hobbylock* models (Lesson 28). The foot can also be used when serging over wire (Lessons 7 and 24) and for serging over trim (Lesson 27) or cording (Lesson 4).

Fig. 1-12: *The ribbon foot positions trim or cord for serger application.*

Ribbon foot (Fig. 1-12)—Available for all *Hobbylock* models, the ribbon foot is specially designed to guide ribbon, tape, or cording when serging over it. Especially applicable for serging over trim (Lesson 27), this foot also works well for serge-cording (Lesson 4).

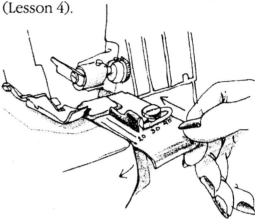

Fig. 1-13: *The workpiece guide plate on the 797 is a looper cover and work support.*

Workpiece guide plate (Fig. 1-13)—Available on the 797 model only, this plate acts as a looper cover and work support when using the 2-thread double chainstitch. The movable guide on the plate can be adjusted to a specific width or can be removed entirely to allow chainstitching at any distance from an edge.

Standard Hobbylock *accessories*—All *Hobbylock* sergers come with a packet of useful accessories. These are listed in your manual and include: tweezers for easy threading, oil and a lint brush for regular maintenance, thread nets and thread unreeling discs (spool caps) for smooth feeding of thread, and a spare knife and needles for convenience. Also included are a presser foot used for the narrow rolled edge, screwdrivers, and a special needle change tool. Refer to your manual for detailed information.

Loving Care

Your serger is a precision instrument. If you treat it well, it will reward you with years of ornamental serging. But without proper care, it can create problems on even the simplest project.

You may not be taking your sewing machine in for regular checkups, but for your serger regular checkups are essential. The serger's timing and accuracy need to be much more finely tuned than the sewing machine's.

Follow these basic guidelines to keep your serger running smoothly: (Fig. 1-14)

After Every Project

_____ Remove the presser foot, needle plate, and needle(s).

_____ Remove **large pieces of lint** with a fluffed-out lint brush.

_____ Blow out **fine lint** with environmentally safe pressurized air, a hair dryer, a computer vacuum or a household vacuum on reversed air flow. OR...

_____ Use a lint brush lightly dipped in sewing machine oil to remove **fine lint** particles. The oil also provides some gentle lubrication.

N **Note:** Never blow into your serger to remove lint particles. The small amount of moisture in your breath can harm your machine.

At least every third project

_____ Change the needle(s).

■ Use the correct type and size of needle for your fabric.

■ Push the needle(s) all the way up into the needle bar, using the needle change tool.

At least every 12 to 15 hours of serging

_____ Oil your serger. See your manual: a few key spots should be oiled every time you begin a project. Other moving parts need not be oiled as often. Use only sewing machine oil.

_____ If your serger is noisier than usual, oil it.

_____ If you haven't used your serger for several months, **always** oil it before using it again.

_____ After oiling, test-serge on scraps of fabric to remove any residual oil.

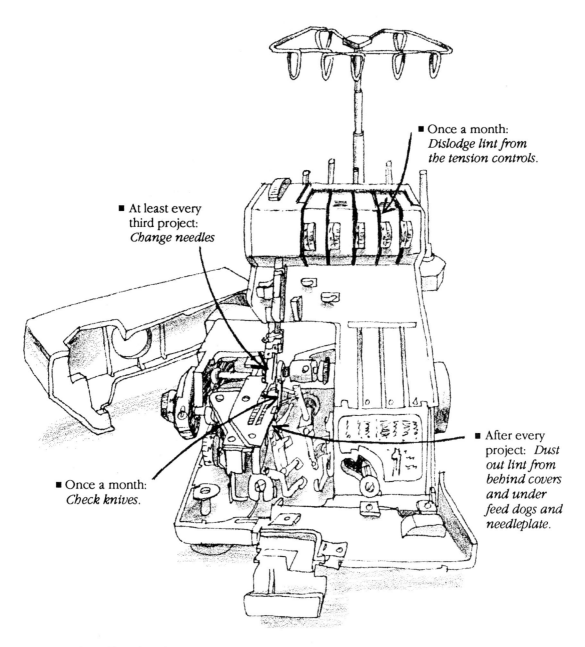

- Once a month: *Dislodge lint from the tension controls.*

- At least every third project: *Change needles*

- After every project: *Dust out lint from behind covers and under feed dogs and needleplate.*

- Once a month: *Check knives.*

Fig. 1-14: *Follow these basic guidelines to keep your serger running smoothly.*
- At least every 12-15 serging hours: *Oil as instructed in your manual.*
- Once a year: *Take your serger to your local dealer for a checkup.*

Once a Month

____ Remove lint lodged in the tension controls.

■ Open the cover and brush out dust and lint from the tension discs or:

■ Turn the tension controls to -5.

■ Open the cover and put knotted thread through each tension control.

■ Reset the tensions to normal and pull the knotted thread back and forth through the controls to remove any lint.

■ Close the cover.

____ Check the knives.

■ Do they cut ragged edges?

■ Do they have a shiny, worn look?

■ If so, replace one or both knives (refer to your manual for instructions or see your local dealer).

Once a Year

____ Take your serger to your local dealer for an annual checkup.

____ Stock up on needles, new accessories, and the latest books and information.

2. Ornamental Serging Basics

- Tension—The Key to Success
- Decorative Threads
- Threads Other Than Decorative
- Shaping Materials
- Other Important Serging Supplies
- Ornamental Serging Sample Book
- Exploring Your Machine's Creative Limits

Tension—The Key to Success

Once you have a thorough knowledge of serger tension adjustment, you will be able to use your machine to its fullest creative potential. On your sewing machine, you would change the tension only if there were something wrong with the stitch. *On a serger, you will readjust your tension settings often due to differences in thread, fabric, or stitch type.* You will also change tensions as you change the stitch length and width and when you want to create varied effects.

Although tension adjustment is part of any basic serger instruction, we will cover it again because it is such a critical part of ornamental serging.

Changing serger tension settings is not complicated if you follow a few basic guidelines and know what a correctly adjusted stitch should look like. In a balanced 3-thread overlock stitch, the looper threads should hug the top and bottom of the fabric and overlock exactly on the edge. The needle thread should form a line along the left edge of the stitch and look like sewing machine straight-stitching on both top and bottom. (Fig. 2-1)

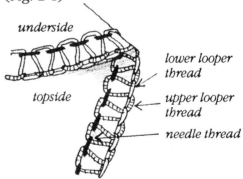

underside

topside

lower looper thread

upper looper thread

needle thread

Fig. 2-1: *When tension settings are balanced, the looper threads will hug the top and bottom of the fabric and overlock exactly on the cut edge.*

See your manual or refer back to pages 5 - 10 for examples of perfectly balanced tension for all the stitch options on your *Hobbylock* model.

Practicing tension adjustment

If you have never experimented with your machine's tension settings, or if you have any doubt about how to adjust the serger tension properly, try this experiment:

1. Thread your serger with different colors of all-purpose or serger thread. (For easier identification, you may want to use the same colors as those on your thread guides.) If you have a 4- or 5-thread machine, adjust for a 3-thread overlock stitch and test that first. Later you can convert to other stitch configurations and test them as well. Adjust for a medium-length (standard N), balanced stitch.

2. Put all the tension dials on the standard N settings. If you tend to forget which control adjusts which looper or needle, label them with small pieces of masking tape. Study your manual and place each label on the correct control until you know it by heart.

3. Set the lower looper tension all the way to -5. At this point, the lower looper is at the loosest tension. Leave the upper looper and needle tension on the N setting.

4. Cut two 4" by 6" rectangles from medium-weight woven fabric. Serge-seam the rectangles together along one side and examine the results. Learn what the lower looper thread looks like when the tension is at its lowest (loosest) setting. Label and save your seam sample for your sample book (see page 30).

5. Set your lower looper tension almost (but not quite) all the way to +5, the highest (tightest) setting. Leave the upper looper and needle tensions at the N setting. Repeat step 4, checking the results of a tightened lower looper tension. Label and save your sample.

6. Turn the lower looper tension back to the standard N setting and loosen the upper looper tension all the way to the -5. Leave the lower looper and needle tension on the N settings. Repeat step 4, checking the results of a loosened upper looper tension. Label and save your sample.

7. Repeat step 5 for the upper looper by tightening the tension and leaving the lower looper and needle tensions on the center settings.

Balancing the tension

Now you are beginning to understand the effects of changing the tension settings on your serger—and you're no longer afraid to experiment! The next step is to learn how to adjust for a balanced tension:

1. Set the tension controls to the standard N settings.

2. Cut long 4"-wide strips from medium-weight woven fabric for testing. Put the right sides of two long strips together and serge a test seam for a few inches on the long edge.

3. Stop and look at the stitching behind the presser foot without removing the fabric. Look at the upper and lower looper threads. Remember, the looper threads should meet at the edge. If one thread is pulled *over* the edge, the other thread is too tight. First, find the one that appears to be too tight and **loosen** it (toward -1). (Fig. 2-2) Serge a few more inches. If

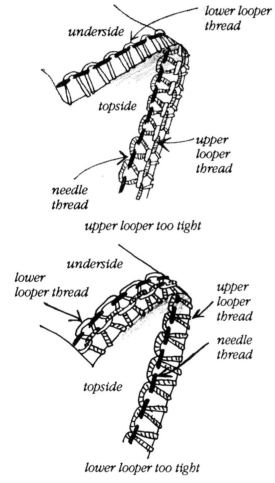

upper looper too tight

lower looper too tight

Fig. 2-2: *Find the looper tension that is too tight and loosen it.*

the tension hasn't been eased or has been made worse, return the control to the original position and **tighten** the other looper thread (the one that appears to be too loose) by turning it toward +1. Continue to test-serge and adjust—a few inches at a time—until the looper tensions are balanced.

4. Examine the needle-thread line from the right side. If it is too loose, the seamline will pull open. If it is too tight, the seamline will pucker. (Fig. 2-3) The needle-thread tension won't

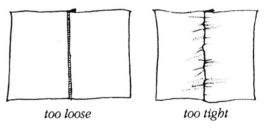

too loose   too tight

Fig. 2-3: *When the needle tension is too loose, the seamline will pull open. When the needle tension is too tight, the seamline will pucker.*

always need to be adjusted. Change the needle tension only if the seamline pulls open or looks puckered. Turn it to a plus number to tighten the tension or a minus number to loosen it.

Follow these guidelines to get perfectly balanced tension every time:

1. Adjust one control at a time and test-serge after each adjustment. Don't make the mistake of turning all the tension controls at the same time.

2. Make only small adjustments. A small adjustment can make a big difference. (For normal, balanced serging, the *Hobbylock* usually needs very little adjustment.)

3. When adjusting the looper tension, first loosen the looper thread that appears to be too tight. If the adjustment doesn't seem to help the problem, or if it makes it worse, *put that control back where it was* and tighten the other looper tension. Continue adjusting, one control at a time (putting the setting back where you started if the change did not help), until the tension is balanced.

4. Every time you use a different type of thread or fabric, you will need to check your tension adjustments. For the most accurate adjustments, test-serge on scraps of the actual project fabric, using the same grain and the same number of layers.

Continue to practice, test, and experiment with varying fabrics and tensions. Learn to recognize what happens when you make tension adjustments. As you proceed through this book, you will find that *some very interesting novelty stitches can be formed by varying the tensions*. Both the rolled-edge stitch and flatlocking are created with tension adjustments. And that's only the beginning of a wide range of possibilities.

Confidence in using your serger and the ability to use it to its full potential come only after you are comfortable with changing tensions.

Decorative Threads

We're constantly learning about new or newly discovered threads, yarns, ribbons, and trims that can be serged ornamentally. Creative serger enthusiasts have used everything from elastic thread to fine wire to create special ornamental effects.

Many materials for decorative serging can be found in the notions and trim departments of your local fabric store. Also try sewing machine dealerships; needlecraft, yarn, and craft shops; and mail-order sources.

Follow these thread selection guidelines as a starting point to test your ornamental serging possibilities:

Decorative Serging Quick Reference Chart

Use: N - Needle
UL - Upper Looper
LL - Lower Looper
SO - Serge Over
A - All Uses

EASE:
* Easy
** Moderate
*** Challenging

Tension Adjustment: N - None
S - Slight
L - Lots

TYPE	SIZES AND COLORS AVAILABLE	USE	EASE OF USE	TENSION ADJUST- MENT	SUBSTI- TUTE	DESCRIPTION	APPLICATION	NOTES
Buttonhole Twist	Variety of colors.	A	*	N-S		Slightly heavier than all-purpose thread.	Edging or flatlock seaming all types sportswear, home decorator items.	May work satisfactorily in size 14 needle, not in size 11.
Woolly Nylon	Variety, including variegated.	A	*	S		Crimped, yarn-like thread, stretchy, fluffs up when serged. May melt with hot iron.	Excellent for rolled edge, other decorative edges, and flatlocking. Soft elastic seams on lingerie, swimwear, activewear.	May be used through needle. Tensions may need to be adjusted. Best coverage of any lightweight decorative thread.
Rayon	Variety of colors and sizes, including new "pearl" rayon.	A	*	N-S-L (depend- ing on size)		Shiny, silk-like thread, smooth, bright colors.	High-luster edging or flatlock seaming for elegant fashion garments and accessories.	
Silk	Variety of colors and sizes.	A	*	N-S	Rayon Threads, Machine Embroidery	Shiny, soft, smooth, expensive.	High-luster edging or flatlock seaming for elegant fashion garments and accessories.	
Metallics	Variety of sizes and colors, including variegated.	A	**	S-L		Adds glitter, can be used multi-strand or combined with other threads.	Highly decorative edge for sportswear, eveningwear, holiday gifts, and home decor.	Vary greatly according to manufacturer. Avoid those with coarse, metal fibers. Experiment to find which works best.
Braids	Variety of sizes, colors and fibers.	UL, LL, SO	** to ***	L		Purchase by the yard.	Edging or flatlocking of garments, accessories, home decorator, and nursery items.	Require testing and experiments to achieve tension balance. It may be necessary to bypass tension disc altogether. Use in loopers only.

Decorative Serging Quick Reference Chart

Ribbon	Variety of colors, fibers, including silk, acrylic, polyester. 1/16 – 1/4" wide.	UL, LL, SO	***	L	Braided Rayon Ribbon	Soft knitting ribbon, bright colors.	Edging or flatlocking of garments, accessories, home decorator, and nursery items.	Require testing and experimentation to achieve tension balance. It may be necessary to bypass tension disc altogether. Use in loopers only.
Braided Rayon Ribbon (Ribbon Floss)	Variety of colors, including metallic. 1/8" wide.	UL, LL, SO	**	L		Soft knitting ribbon, bright colors crosswound on tube.	Edging or flatlocking of garments, accessories, home decorator, and nursery items.	Require testing and experimentation to achieve tension balance. It may be necessary to bypass tension disc altogether. Use in loopers only.
Crochet Thread	Variety of colors, including variegated and metallic.	UL, LL, SO	** to ***	L		Available in acrylic and cotton, strong thread.	Edging or flatlocking of garments, accessories, home decorator, and nursery items.	Require testing and experimentation to achieve tension balance. It may be necessary to bypass tension disc altogether. Use in loopers only.
Pearl Cotton	Variety of colors and sizes—#5 and 8 are most common.	UL, LL, SO	#8 ** #5 ***	L	Crochet thread, Rayon "pearl"	Soft, shiny, tightly twisted, strong thread.	Edging or flatlocking of garments, accessories, home decorator, and nursery items.	Require testing and experimentation to achieve tension balance. It may be necessary to bypass tension disc altogether. Use in loopers only.
Yarns	Variety of colors. Two- or three-ply. Baby or Sport yarn.	UL, LL, SO	*** (Two-ply easiest)	L	Pearl cotton, Woolly nylon	Soft, smooth, tightly twisted.	Edging or flatlocking of garments, accessories, home decorator, and nursery items.	Require testing and experimentation to achieve tension balance. It may be necessary to bypass tension disc altogether. Use in loopers only.
Monofilament Nylon	Very fine. Clear or smoke color. Variety of weights—#60 and #80 (finer) are common.	N, UL, LL (Use finer weights for needle.)	*	N		Strong, invisible thread, used with decorative thread, may melt with hot iron. The higher the number, the finer the thread.	Fashion accessories, home decorator items requiring strong seams, thread invisibility.	Some brands are too heavy and wiry to loop well. Look for lightweight, supple selection.
Elastic	Various sizes, including 1/4 – 3/8" widths.	A SO-1/4" & 3/8" widths	*	S		Adds stability. Used for shirring.		
Machine Embroidery, Lingerie	Variety of colors.	N, UL	**	N-S		Lightweight, smooth, delicate.	Lingerie, lightweight fabrics where stress is not a factor. Edging soft fabrics.	Pfaff's Mez Alcazar is in this category.

Special Tip: Decorative threads crosswound on top-feeding cones are the easiest to use. (Fig. 2-4) Those wound in

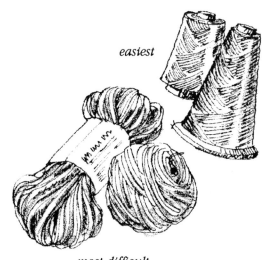

easiest

most difficult

Fig. 2-4: *Crosswound decorative thread is easiest to use. Balls and skeins are more difficult.*

balls or skeins or sold by the yard are more difficult because they require extra care in order to help them feed evenly when serging.

Not all decorative threads will serge successfully in every machine. It's important always to test first. Allow at least seven yards for each looper you'll be testing and two yards for each needle. When estimating actual project yardage required, you will need 10 times the finished decorative serging length for each looper.

Serging decorative threads

You have three options when serging with decorative threads: threading it through the loopers, threading it through the needle, or serging over it.

Most often the decorative thread is threaded through the upper looper. This part of the stitch shows on the top side as you are serging. On a rolled edge (page 54) or reversible-edge binding (page 66), the upper looper should be the only thread visible on either side.

If you want a balanced stitch (identical on both top and bottom), you will also need to thread the lower looper with decorative thread. In some cases, when the thread is not strong, the lower looper will not be able to handle a thread that works in the upper looper. This is because the upper looper thread has less movement in the thread guides and a shorter distance between the spool and the presser foot, so less stress is put on the thread.

The loopers don't pass through the fabric, so they both have larger eyes than a serger needle. This makes it possible to use thicker thread or yarn in your loopers. Consider these questions in determining whether a thread or yarn will work in the serger loopers:

Puffed Serged·Braid Frogs

Thread·Chain Tassels

Double·Bound Seams

Fig. 1: *This high-fashion fall outfit is ornamented with shiny black rayon thread, serged into a decorative frog and eye-catching tassels (Chapter 8) as well as show-stopping double-bound seams (Chapter 3).*

Serge-Pleated Fabric

Decorative Exposed Seams

Serged Trim

Fig. 2: *Nubby beige fabric becomes a major fashion statement with the addition of taupe ornamental serging. Woolly nylon thread is used to ornament the collar fabric (Chapter 8), for basic decorative seams (Chapter 3), and to add serged trim to the collar edge (Chapter 5).*

Fig. 3: *Casual sportswear need not be plain. Black fringe emphasizes a yoke (Chapter 8) and coordinating serged-fold self braid (Chapter 5) adorns the neckline. A lapped and top-stitched zipper (Chapter 7) with matching fringe turns the utilitarian bag into a special creation.*

Serged-Fold Self-Braid

Thread-Chain Fringe

Lapped & Top-stitched Zipper

Serger Cutwork

Double Rolled Edge

Serged Appliqué

Fig. 4: *Crisp and fresh, this pretty dress shows off three unusual serging techniques. The bib collar is bordered with a double rolled edge (Chapter 4) and accented with serger cutwork (Chapter 8). The handbag is ornamented with coordinating serger appliqué (also Chapter 8).*

Flat-locked Fringe

Fig. 5: A businesslike suit is spiced up easily by adding serged piping (Chapter 5), serge-bound buttonholes (Chapter 7), and a focal-point tie with flatlocked-fringe edges (Chapter 6).

Serged Piping

Serge-Bound Buttonholes

Elasticized
Trim

Corded
Flatlocking

Elasticized
Binding

Fig. 6: *This solid-color swimsuit sports
ornamental serging to make it anything but
ordinary. Corded flatlocking (Chapter 6)
highlights the trunk portion. Contrasting
elasticized binding keeps the legs securely in
place and elasticized trim repeats the black
accent color at the neckline (both Chapter 5).*

Serged Cording

Serged Couching

Thread-Chain Cording & Tassels

Fig. 7: *Casual clothes are a perfect backdrop for ornamental serging skills. Serge-couching (Chapter 6) and matching serge-cording (Chapter 4) accent this bright red top. Serger thread-chain bracelets (Chapter 8) pull the look together.*

Balanced
Decorative
Edges

Serged
Button Loops

Fishline Ruffles

Fig. 8: *Even elegant evening wear can be enhanced with special serger techniques. Serged elastic button loops (Chapter 7), a balanced decorative edge (Chapter 4), and fluffy fishline ruffles (Chapter 6) are all featured in a coordinating metallic thread.*

1. When folded over double-layer, will the decorative thread easily pass through the looper eye? (Fig. 2-5)

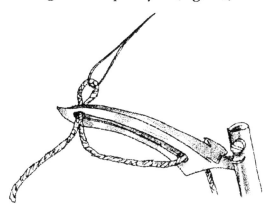

Fig. 2-5: Be sure your decorative thread or yarn will easily pass through the looper eye when it is doubled.

2. Is the thread flexible enough to form a uniform stitch without catching in the loopers?

3. Is the thread smooth or tightly twisted enough to ensure trouble-free feeding and prevent fraying or snagging?

4. Is the thread yardage continuous and long enough to complete the project? (Always allow an extra 8 to 10 yards for testing.)

Some lightweight threads also fit through the needle eye. Woolly nylon, fine metallic thread, lightweight monofilament nylon, and top-stitching thread are examples. These threads therefore can be used for the ladder side of flatlocking (see page 45) or for other stitches that require loosened needle tension. In many cases, though, you will not need decorative thread in the needle, so use all-purpose or serger thread.

If a yarn, ribbon, or trim is too heavy or wide to fit through a looper or needle, you have the option of serging over it. To do this, make sure that the stitch you use is wide enough to cover the trim without stitching into it. You also have the option of using a 3-thread balanced, rolled-edge, or flatlock stitch, so test first for the best results.

When serging over a narrow trim, use a ribbon foot or insert the trim under the back of the presser foot and over the front. Make sure the trim fits to the right of the needle and to the left of the knife. Turn the handwheel to begin, and form 1" to 2" of stitches over the trim before inserting the fabric. (Fig. 2-6)

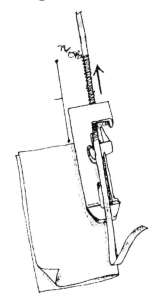

Fig. 2-6: Serge over trim for 1" to 2" before inserting the fabric.

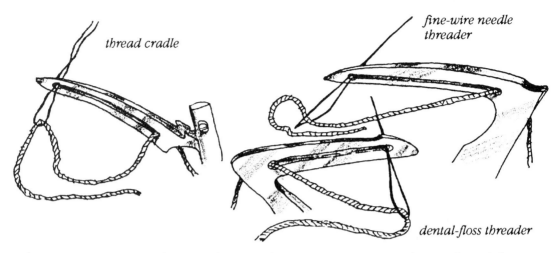

thread cradle

fine-wire needle threader

dental-floss threader

Fig. 2-7: *Here are options for easily threading heavy or limp decorative threads through looper eyes.*

Always serge slowly (set the foot control at half speed). To highlight the trim rather than the stitching, use monofilament nylon or matching lightweight serger thread in the upper looper.

If the trim is bulky, use the beading foot or remove the presser foot and guide the trim manually between the needle and the knife. Hold both the trim and the fabric taut. As we discuss corded edgings and other techniques requiring serging over threads or strands, we'll give more specific instructions for successful results.

Special threading tips

To begin, clip the thread you are using above the spool and tie on the decorative thread. Bypass the tension control to prevent the knot from breaking or untying as it is pulled through. Pull the knot through the remaining thread guides. You may have to clip the knot at the eye of the looper or needle and thread it through manually.

Heavy or limp decorative threads are difficult to thread through the looper eyes. Serger pros use several tricks to do the job easily. Naomi makes a thread cradle by looping a strand of all-purpose thread around the specialty thread and then threads the ends of the all-purpose thread through the eye. (Fig. 2-7) Tammy uses a dental-floss threader (available at any drugstore) for the same purpose. Fine-wire needle threaders are also available from sewing retailers and mail-order sources to simplify the threading process.

Rethread the tension control and start serging with wide, long stitches. Gradually test and alter the stitch for the desired effect. For the most accurate results, always test on scraps of actual project fabric.

Turn the handwheel a few stitches to make sure the stitches are forming correctly. Then serge slowly for a few inches before stopping to adjust the tension. One general rule to keep in mind: the more resistance a thread has, the less tension it needs to have exerted on it. For example, a rough metallic thread needs less (looser) tension and a smooth, shiny rayon needs more tension.

If the tension is too tight after adjusting it all the way, check to be sure the thread isn't hanging up on a thread guide. If it is still too tight, remove the thread from the tension control. Place a strip of transparent tape over the tension slot to keep the thread out. (Fig. 2-8) Or, remove the

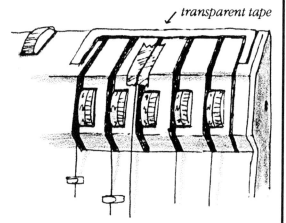

transparent tape

Fig. 2-8: If the tension is too tight, place transparent tape over the slot to keep the thread out.

thread from the tension disc and set the dial at +5. The thread will have more resistance on it than with the tape method, but it should remain out from between the discs.

Special Tip: Tensions and stitch length can vary from machine to machine, even on the same model. Your dealer cannot expand the range but can adjust the range slightly in one direction or the other.

Adjust to the desired stitch length. Most decorative seams and edges are serged with a very short, "satin" stitch length. There should be enough thread coverage so little, if any, fabric shows through the serging. But, **if you adjust the serger for too short a stitch length, the fabric may jam under the presser foot** or the seam may pucker. To be safe, we usually begin with a standard N stitch length (especially for heavier decorative thread) and adjust toward a shorter length as far as necessary for the most attractive satin stitch. The thickness of the thread and the type of fabric you use will determine how short a stitch length you need. Finer thread requires a shorter stitch length for maximum coverage, while heavier thread looks better with a slightly longer stitch length. (Fig. 2-9)

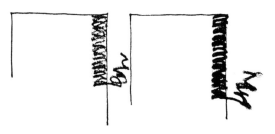

short stitch length— finer thread

longer stitch length— heavier thread

Fig. 2-9: For maximum coverage, use a shorter stitch length when using finer thread. Lengthen the stitch slightly for heavier thread.

When shortening the stitch length, you will also need to tighten both looper tensions or the stitching will hang off the edge of the fabric. (Fig. 2-10)

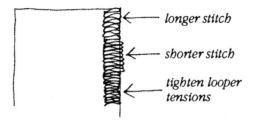

Fig. 2-10: *Tighten both looper tensions when shortening the stitch so stitches won't hang off the edge.*

Because decorative stitching is an important part of the design of a garment or project, the stitches must be smooth and uniform. The slightest pulling of the decorative thread can narrow the stitch or even break the strand. (Fig. 2-11)

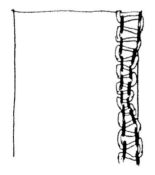

Fig. 2-11: *Stitches will narrow or break if the decorative thread does not feed evenly.*

If uneven stitches are a problem, check for anything that may be causing uneven feeding of your decorative thread. One common problem is that the thread catches on the spool itself (prevented by using a thread-unreeling disc from the accessory kit) or winds around the spool pin under the spool. Make sure the thread is feeding evenly off the spool.

Use thread nets to control feeding of slippery or wiry thread. For threads wound on balls or skeins, rewind the thread loosely by hand onto empty cones or spools. Rewind thread and yarn quickly with a cone-winder, sold in knitting shops.

Some serger pros prefer simply reeling off several yards at a time from the ball or skein while serging. With this method, be sure that the feeding is not impeded by sewing tools cluttering your work area.

To illustrate how important even feeding can be, our serging friend Sue Green-Baker tells an amusing story. As she was working with decorative yarn in her upper looper, she kept getting uneven stitches (which she calls hiccups) in her serging. After checking all the usual trouble spots, she discovered that her kitten was playing with the ball of yarn on the floor. Even though she was reeling off extra yarn as she serged, the kitten's pulling occasionally caused just enough tension change to create major glitches in her otherwise perfect decorative stitching.

Combining thread types

You may need to make additional tension adjustments when you combine different thread types and use them in the same looper simultaneously. We do this for special decorative effects, such as adding a shiny fine metallic thread to woolly nylon or for toning down the color blocking of a variegated thread using one solid-color thread or another strand of the same thread with the colors aligned differently. Another thread commonly combined with a decorative one is fine elastic thread, because it adds stretch-prevention to serged edges and seams.

When combining thread types, make sure both are feeding evenly without restrictions. You may need to adjust the tension or remove one of the threads from the tension control. Always test first before serging your actual project.

Pressing over decorative thread

Some types of decorative thread (such as woolly nylon, monofilament nylon, and pearl cotton) are sensitive to a hot iron. For best results, use a press cloth to prevent melting or a permanent shine on your thread.

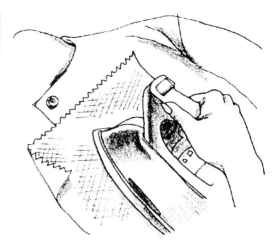

Fig. 2-12: *Use a press cloth to prevent melting or shine with sensitive decorative thread.*

(Fig. 2-12) Consider the fiber content of the thread and treat it similarly to a fabric of the same type. If in doubt, test first.

Threads Other Than Decorative

All-purpose or serger thread: All-purpose thread is most often cotton-covered polyester, wound parallel on conventional spools. Serger thread usually has the same fiber content but is a little lighter in weight than all-purpose thread. It is crosswound on cones or tubes so that it will feed more evenly, in an upward direction, during higher-speed serger sewing.

Monofilament nylon thread: Used for many serger techniques, this handy thread comes in either clear or smoke shades. We prefer the lighter-weight size 80 thread for use in either the needle or loopers. Monofilament nylon is practically invisible for covering serger-applied trims and for "floating" stitches on top of the fabric. Because the nylon also is strong, you can use it in the lower looper for tightening down a rolled edge or for perfecting other techniques. Be careful to prevent melting this thread when pressing.

Fusible thread: A special thread combined with a heat-activated component, this exciting product bonds easily at the touch of a steam iron (much like fusible interfacing). Fusible thread helps stabilize and position edges and seam allowances in a wide variety of decorative techniques. We also use it to position serged braid or cord for couching and monogramming. Always test your application first on your project scraps.

Although top-stitching may be added for extra security, the pliable fusible thread bond withstands both washing and dry cleaning. For maximum fusing coverage, we usually use it in the lower looper of a 3- or 4-thread serged stitch. The more fusible thread exposed, the better the bond. When you use this thread in the lower looper, tighten the tension slightly so the thread does not extend past the edge of the fabric.

Always press from the top side of the stitching. Never allow the iron to touch the fusible thread directly. Because the fusible component has a low melting point, press-baste first with a warm iron. Then permanently bond using as much steam and heat as your fabric will tolerate. Allow the bond to cool before moving the fabric. Also, quickly secure seam ends with a shot of steam applied over (but not touching) the thread chain.

Shaping Materials

Clear elastic: About one-third the thickness of regular elastic, clear polyurethane elastic does not "grow" as it is stitched through. It is also impervious to nicks from serger knives. Handy for many sewing and serging projects, it comes in five widths—1/8", 1/4", 3/8", 1/2", and 3/4".

Elastic thread: Available in a range of colors and sizes (from lightweight to cording), elastic thread has several interesting serger applications. All but the heaviest weights can be threaded through the loopers (see Lesson 34, Serged Elastic Button Loops, page 152). Elastic thread can also be used to create shirring or to stabilize an edge.

Fishline: If you don't already have some on hand, fishline is available at most sporting goods, discount, and drug stores. We use it for decoratively ruffling edges. Choose the clear line to avoid show-through in your project. Fishline weights vary from 12 lb. to 40 lb. Use the 12 lb. for light-weight fabrics and a heavier weight for heavier fabrics, when serging over two layers, or for extra body.

Fine wire: Wire, used to shape ornamental edges, is available in any craft store. Fine, lightweight floral wire is usually precut to 18" lengths. For projects that require longer lengths, try beading wire, which comes on spools and in a variety of colors and weights.

Batting: Various weights of batting are available in both cotton and polyester. We prefer either bonded batting, which holds together well, or fleece, which is a little thinner.

Fiberfill: This shredded batting is most often polyester and is used to stuff pillows and in craft projects.

Other Important Serging Supplies

- Your *Hobbylock* serger
- Your owner's manual and all machine attachments and accessories (including tweezers and screwdrivers)
- Optional accessory feet
- A straight-stitch sewing machine, preferably with zigzag capability

- Needle-nosed pliers or needle inserter
- Extra needles
- Extra knives (one comes with your serger)
- Fine-wire needle threader or dental-floss threader
- Thread nets (some are included with your machine)
- Thread unreeling discs (spool caps)
- Seam sealant like *Fray Check*
- Washable glue stick or fabric glue (such as Aileen's *OK to Wash-It* or Magic American's *Fabric Mender Magic*)
- Fusible transfer web (such as *Wonder-Under*)
- Stabilizers—both water-soluble (such as *Solvy* or *Wash-Away*) and tear-away
- Dressmaker shears
- Rotary cutter and mat
- Seam ripper
- Yardstick
- Tape measure
- Water-soluble and air-erasable marking pens
- Machine lint brush or canned air
- Loop turner, darning needle, or crochet hook
- Any other favorite sewing supplies

Fig. 2-13: Keep a sample book of notes, test results, and creative ideas.

Ornamental Serging Sample Book

We recommend that you keep a sample book of all your lesson results and other testing for later reference. One perfect way to do this is to use a *Hobbylock* workbook (available for all models) and add extra pages for additional samples. (Fig. 2-13) Or use a standard 3-ring binder with heavy paper to mount your finished samples.

Be sure to note your tension, stitch width, and stitch-length settings for each type of stitch, thread, and fabric used. This information will be handy as a starting point for your future projects.

Put creative ideas in your sample book, too. Clip magazine photos, write notes about techniques to try, and add special instructions that come with new types of thread or other ornamental serging supplies. Refer to your sample book for inspiration and information while planning and completing each new serger project.

Exploring Your Machine's Creative Limits

As you work through this book, you will no doubt come up with bright ideas of your own. Because serger sewing is a relatively new art, there are lots of techniques and ideas yet to be discovered and developed.

Be open to experimentation. Test new serger techniques. (Check the "Serger Update" newsletter for the latest ones.) Think about how you can adapt them for your own use. Then take time to answer the following questions in order to inspire your creative efforts:

1. *How can I adapt new sewing products and threads for serger use?* With so many recent technical advances, new serging possibilities abound. Fusible thread (page 28) opened up a wealth of new techniques for us. Clear elastic and elastic thread (page 28) add even more options. Interesting new decorative threads (pages 19-23) continue to be introduced.

2. *How can I combine craft products and ideas with my serging skills?* Many of our latest techniques and projects have come from using craft items such as fine wire (Lesson 7), water-soluble stabilizer (Lesson 37), and beads (Lesson 28).

3. *Can I convert sewing techniques for the serger in order to speed up a project or make it more durable?* Fishline ruffles (Lesson 6), lettuced edges (Lesson 5), and French seams (Lesson 1) are a breeze with the help of a serger.

4. *Are there unique stitch configurations on the serger that I can use for unusual ornamental effects?* Serged lace (Lesson 24), reversible-edge binding (lesson 8), and serger chain art (Lesson 35) were all developed because of the machine's unique stitching capabilities.

5. *Is there another way to manipulate an edge or a fold to get a different result?* Double-bound seams (Lesson 2) and edges (Lesson 13) and double rolled edges (Lessons 5 and 17) are some recent options.

6. *Can I copy a trim or decorative effect from ready-to-wear?* Look in stores, magazines, and catalogs for inspiration. Check out crafts projects, too.

The more you use your serger and experiment with all its ornamental options, the easier you will find it is to be creative and to develop ideas of your own. So start now to explore all the possibilities and really use your *Hobbylock* to its creative limits.

3. Decorative Seams

- **Lesson 1. Basic Seams**
- **Lesson 2. Serge-bound Seams**
- **Lesson 3. Flatlocked Seams**

Serging seams is one of the most basic uses for your serger. The type of fabric, the amount of stress placed on the seam during wearing, and personal preference are all factors in selecting which seam to use.

Any seam may be hidden on the inside or used ornamentally, exposed on the right side of the fabric. Exposed seams are especially popular on many of today's sportier ready-to-wear garments.

When seams are exposed, they become a decorative design element. Therefore, the tension and stitches must be perfect, no matter what kind of thread you use. Always test first with two layers of the project fabric and the same thread you will be using. Compare your samples with the illustrations of perfect stitch formation in your manual or on pages 5, 9, and 10, and adjust accordingly.

When serging decorative seams, the method you use to secure seam ends is important. When a seam will be crossed by another serged seam, we usually don't secure the ends by any other method. The serged thread chains hold the ends in place until they can be seamed across and secured. If additional reinforcement is needed, we straight-stitch along the

needleline of the second seam for about 2" to 3" across the first seam. (Fig. 3-1)

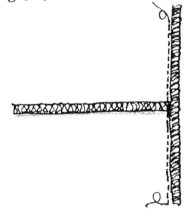

Fig. 3-1: *Serged seams are often secured by another seam. Straight-stitching can add reinforcement.*

When the seam ends will not be crossed and secured with a second serged seam, they must be secured with another method. The deciding factor is usually how much the method of securing will show. Because exposed seams are on the outside of the fabric and not worn next to the skin, our first choice is to use a drop of seam sealant on the ends. Be sure to let the sealant dry thoroughly before cutting the chain.

Special Tip: If the wet seam sealant accidentally touches another part of the project, leaving a stain, rub the spot with a cotton swab soaked in rubbing alcohol. The stain will disappear.

Lesson 1.
Basic Seams

When seaming, it is important to serge-trim some of the fabric, even if it is just enough to neaten the edges. This ensures even stitching, neater edges, and better control of the width trimmed. You'll find it easiest to trim between 1/8" and 3/8".

A basic serged seam can be sewn with either a 3-, 3/4-, or 5-thread stitch. If the seam will not be top- or edge-stitched but you want the seam to be as secure as possible, use a 3/4- or 5-thread stitch or straight-stitch along the needleline after serging a 3-thread seam.

Basic decorative seam

To serge a decorative, exposed seam, place the fabric wrong sides together and serge with the needle on the seamline. (When using two needles, the left needle will be on the seamline.) When both sides of the seam will show, use the same type of thread in both the upper and lower loopers. You may decide to use the same color for both loopers or to vary the colors to achieve a desired effect. Depending on the seam placement, you may not need to press (see our Double-Bow Pillow project, page 37).

Exposed seams are often pressed to one side and top-stitched for neatness or to add strength. In this case, only the seam's upper looper thread will show. Apply top-stitching right next to the overlocked edge using a long stitch length. For better accuracy, use the blindhem foot on your sewing machine to guide your stitching evenly. Adjust the foot so that the overlocked edge is next to the guide. (Fig. 3-2)

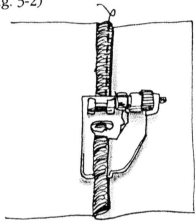

Fig. 3-2: *Use a sewing machine blindhem foot to top-stitch the decorative seam to one side.*

To secure an exposed seam quickly, put fusible thread (see page 28) in the lower looper when serging the seam. Before serging, determine to which side the seam will be pressed and serge with that side down. Tighten the lower looper tension slightly so the fusible thread does not show from the right side. Serge-seam. Carefully press-baste the seam to the side, then steam thoroughly to permanently fuse. For most seams, no other securing is needed.

Hidden lapped serging technique

We often need to lap decorative stitching—when completing a circle, joining the ends of an opening, or (occasionally) correcting irregular areas of serging. This technique eliminates the need to serge on and off the fabric, which provides a neater (almost invisible) decorative finish.

1. Raise the needle(s) and presser foot and disengage the stitches from the stitch finger.

2. Insert your fabric, positioning the needle(s) on the seamline. If you are joining ends of an opening or correcting irregular serging, position the needle(s) about 1/2" before the end of one side of the opening. (Fig. 3-3)

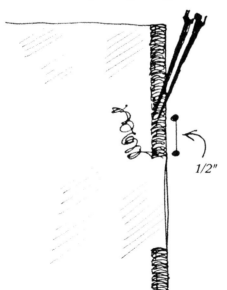

1/2"

Fig. 3-3: *Position the needle(s) 1/2" before the end of the serging when closing an opening or correcting irregular stitching.*

3. Serge until you reach the opposite end of the decorative stitching.

4. Overlap the stitches for 1/2", being careful not to cut the original stitching with your knives.

5. Raise the presser foot and needle(s), clear the stitch finger, and pull the fabric just behind the needle(s). (Fig. 3-4)

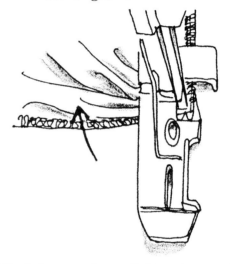

Fig. 3-4: *Raise the needle(s) and presser foot and pull the fabric behind the needle(s).*

6. Serge off to form a thread chain.

7. If you're using a heavy decorative thread, dab on a drop of seam sealant and trim the chain when dry. If you're using a satin stitch and a lighter-weight decorative thread (such as woolly nylon), lapping the stitches should secure them adequately. Simply trim away the excess thread chain after lapping the stitches.

If you are lapping decorative serging and plan to trim the edge, trim away a 2" section of the seam allowance to the serger cutting line where you plan to begin your serging. (Fig. 3-5) Then position the cutting line against the blade before starting.

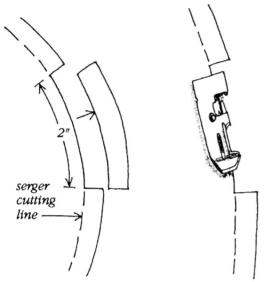

Fig. 3-5: *When trimming the edge, cut away 2" to position the knife on the serger cutting line.*

Reversed decorative seam

This attractive seam features decorative serge-finished allowances that are reversed to the right side of the garment and fused or top-stitched in place.

1. Adjust for a wide, satin-length, balanced 3- or 3/4-thread stitch, using decorative thread in the upper looper, fusible thread in the lower looper, and all-purpose or serger thread in the needle. Tighten the lower looper tension slightly so no fusible thread shows on the top side of the stitching. Test first on project scraps.

2. Decoratively serge-finish both seam edges from the wrong side, positioning the needle (the left needle on a 3/4-thread stitch) on the seamline.

 Special Tip: If your fabric has a tendency to stretch, use a positive differential feed (above 1.0) or ease-plus manually.

3. Reverse the seam allowances to the right side of the garment by straight-stitching them wrong sides together along the needlelines, as shown. (Fig. 3-6) Use a zipper foot for accuracy.

4. Using a press cloth, fuse the allowances to the right side of the fabric on both sides of the seamline.

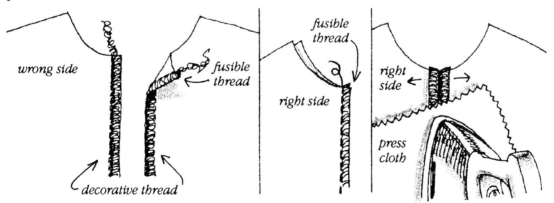

Fig. 3-6: *Serge-finish both edges from the wrong side. Straight-stitch, wrong sides together, along the needlelines. Fuse the allowances to each side.*

Optional: Use all-purpose or serger thread in the lower looper of the decorative stitching instead of fusible thread. After reversing the seam, press and top-stitch the allowances to both sides of the seamline instead of fusing.

Lapped seam

A lapped seam is formed by serge-finishing the edges of both layers of fabric separately, then top-stitching one to the other. Serge-finish both layers with the needle on the seamline. Overlap the edges, matching the seamlines. Top-stitch on the needleline, then top-stitch along the opposite side of the seam if desired. (Fig. 3-7)

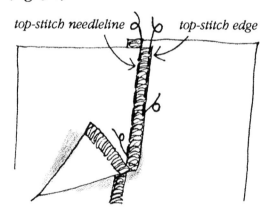

top-stitch needleline   *top-stitch edge*

Fig. 3-7: *For a lapped seam, serge-finish both edges. Top-stitch them together along the needleline. Top-stitch again on the edge if desired.*

Lapped seams are flat and very durable and are also used for reversibles. The upper looper thread on the top fabric layer is the only exposed part of the seam. For reversibles, both layers are serge-finished with one upper looper thread exposed on each side of the garment and top-stitched on the matched needlelines only.

Decorative French seam

Serged French seams on the outside of a garment or project form a decorative detail resembling a tuck. With the fabric right sides together, serge a narrow, medium-length, 3-thread seam. Fold the wrong sides of the fabric over the seam and press carefully. Straight-stitch next to the cut edges, enclosing the seam. Use your sewing machine's blindhem foot to sew a perfectly even width, placing the fold of the seam next to the guide on the foot. This ornamental French seam works best on straight seams. (Fig. 3-8)

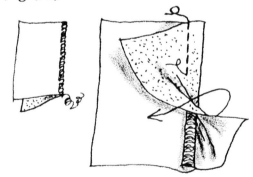

Fig. 3-8: *For an exposed French seam, serge a narrow seam with the right sides together. Wrap the fabric to enclose the serging and straight-stitch.*

Mock flat-felled seam

The mock flat-felled seam, simple yet durable, is used on heavy fabrics. Top-stitching with decorative thread adds ornamental interest to your finished project. Use the widest 5-thread seam, or straight-stitch the seam (right sides together) with a 5/8" seam allowance and serge-finish the edges together using a 3- or 3/4-thread stitch. (Fig. 3-9)

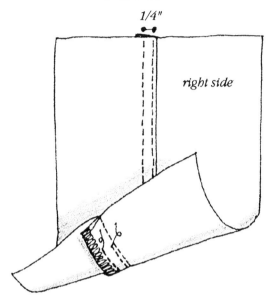

Fig. 3-9: *Create a mock flat-felled seam by serge-finishing wide allowances together, pressing them to one side, and top-stitching.*

Press the allowances to one side. For extra strength, use fusible thread in the lower looper when serge-finishing and fuse the allowances to one side. From the right side, top-stitch over the allowances right next to the seamline and again 1/4" away. Use a long stitch length and a decorative thread like buttonhole twist.

Project: Double-Bow Pillow

Exposed satin-stitched seams become a decorative detail on this attention-getting pillow. It's simple to serge and requires only 3/4 yard of fabric. (Fig. 3-10)

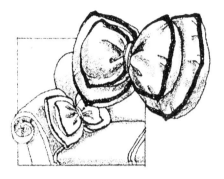

Fig. 3-10: *This double-bow pillow features decorative seams-out detail.*

Foot: Standard
Stitch: 3- or 3/4-thread overlock
Stitch length: Satin
Stitch width: Widest
Thread: Contrasting color to fabric
    Needle(s): All-purpose or serger
    Upper looper: Decorative
    Lower looper: Decorative
Tension: Balanced
Needle(s): Size 11/75
Fabric: 3/4 yard 45"-wide solid or
    print cotton chintz
Notions: Polyester fiberfill

1. Cut two 14" by 20" rectangles, two 12" by 16" rectangles, and one 6-1/2" by 12" rectangle.

2. Adjust your serger for a satin-length, 3- or 3/4-thread overlock stitch. (Fig. 3-11)

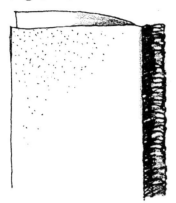

Fig. 3-11: A satin-length overlock stitch forms a pretty, textured seam.

3. Raise the needle(s) and presser foot and clear the stitch finger. Place the two large rectangles wrong sides together. Insert the fabric under the presser foot, positioning the needle(s) on the seamline 2" past the center of one long side (see the hidden lapped serging technique, page 34). Serge-seam all four sides, barely trimming the edges to neaten. Serge on and off at the corners and end the stitching about 5" from the beginning serging. Lightly stuff the pillow with fiberfill and serge-seam the opening closed using the hidden lapped serging technique.

4. Repeat step 3 for the two smaller rectangles.

5. Fold the remaining rectangle in half lengthwise with the wrong sides together. Using a standard N stitch length, serge-seam the long edge. Refold with the seam in the center of the strip and serge-finish both ends.

6. Center the smaller pillow section over the larger one. With the seam underneath, wrap the serged strip from step 5 around the center of both pillows to form a tie. Hand-tack the strip on the back side of the pillow to secure.

Lesson 2. Serge-bound Seams

One of the first things we learn about the serger is that it neatly finishes seams by overlocking the edges. Developing this feature further, we can vary stitch length, width, and thread used to decoratively serge-finish seam allowances. We can also use the serger to speedily encase seam allowances in binding fabric.

Decorative serge-bound seams can be so attractive that we often choose to feature them on the outside of a project. This works especially well for jackets and coats because the seam allowance is featured ornamentally on the outside, while the inside shows only a neat seamline.

A professional-looking binding must be a consistent width. With the serger's exact cutting ability and the even width of its stitches, a consistent-width serged binding is almost foolproof.

Serged seam binding

This decorative seam finish is usually seen on the inside of unlined coats or jackets. It is easily achieved by finishing the seam-allowance edges with decorative, satin-length serging and then sewing the seam with a 5/8" seam allowance. (Fig. 3-12)

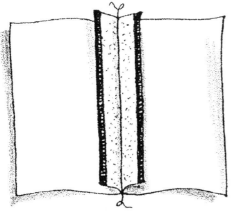

Fig. 3-12: *For serged seam binding, serge-finish the allowance edges with a satin-length stitch before seaming.*

Adjust for a 3-thread stitch. Put a contrasting-color or tone-on-tone decorative thread in the upper looper. Adjust for a short stitch length and a medium to narrow stitch width. Serge-finish from the right side of the fabric, barely skimming the edge. We like to experiment with different stitch widths, depending upon the type of thread we use. Finer thread needs more coverage and looks best with a narrow stitch width. Heavier thread is often more attractive in a wider stitch. Also try woolly nylon or glossy pearl rayon thread for attractive serged seam bindings.

Serged French binding

For a couture effect, add serged French binding to seams using a contrasting or matching strip of fabric. Try combining different types and colors of fabric for stronger emphasis. Nylon *Lycra* works well as binding fabric because it folds tightly against the seam allowance. In addition, its bright colors can add a stunning contrast to dark or neutral fabrics. Try binding velvet with satin, wool with lightweight synthetic suede, or woven fabric with knits.

1. For a finished binding width of approximately 1/4", cut a binding strip 1" wide (four times the desired finished width). The width of the finished binding should be no wider than the width of your serger's widest stitch. If the seams to be bound are straight, the strip can be cut on the crosswise grain. However, if the bound seams are even slightly curved, cut woven strips on the bias or knit strips in the direction of greater stretch (usually crossgrain).

2. Adjust for a 7.5mm stitch width (or the widest on your machine) and a medium stitch length. From the wrong side, with fusible thread in the lower looper, serge-finish one long binding edge, trimming a scant 1/8".

3. Because the binding strip has a narrower seam allowance, it may be easier for you also to pretrim the 5/8" fabric seam allowances to 1/4". Or serge the seam and trim it before applying the binding. As you become more comfortable with the application, you'll be able to serge-seam with a full seam allowance and apply the binding simultaneously. (Fig. 3-13) This one-step method is the easiest and fastest unless the fabric is difficult to manage. If the fabric is rigid,

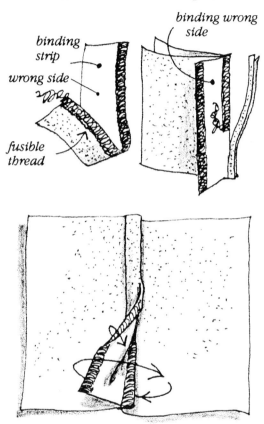

binding strip

binding wrong side

wrong side

fusible thread

Fig. 3-13: For serged French binding, finish the binding-strip edge with fusible thread in the lower looper. Serge-seam the binding and fabric together. Wrap the binding around the seam allowance and fuse it in place.

slippery, or must be held taut while serging, straight-stitch or baste the seam first and trim the seam allowances to 1/4" before applying the binding.

Place the right sides of the fabric together, aligning the binding strip on top over the seamline, fusible side down. (To position serged French binding on the outside of your garment, place the fabric wrong sides together.) Serge-seam the unfinished edges, leaving about a 1/4" seam allowance. The needleline of the serging should be on the seamline of the project. For accuracy, especially if your widest stitch is less than 1/4" wide, straight-stitch at 1/4" and serge-finish the edges together. (Serge-finishing the edges results in a smoother binding.)

If desired, you may change back to serger thread in the lower looper before serge-seaming. Do not stretch while seaming straight binding. For outer curves, ease the binding slightly, and for inner curves stretch it slightly. Wrap the binding smoothly around the seam allowance to encase it. Carefully press-baste to position the binding, then steam-press to fuse securely.

If you are applying a French binding without fusible thread, it is not necessary to serge-finish one long edge of the binding. Serge-seam the binding to the fabric, wrap the binding around the seam allowance, press, and stitch-in-the-ditch. Trim the unfinished long edge of the binding close to the stitching on the underside.

Press the binding to one side and top-stitch next to the folded edge to secure. (Fig. 3-14)

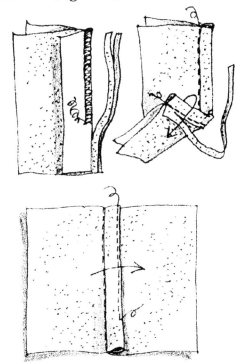

Fig. 3-14: *Make a French binding without fusible thread by serge-seaming the strip to the fabric. Wrap the strip around the seam allowance and stitch-in-the-ditch. Trim the unfinished edge, then top-stitch the binding to one side.*

Double-bound seam

This self-bound seam takes some extra time and skill to construct, but it is very durable and a real show-stopper. Both seam allowances are wrapped with self fabric, then decoratively serged from the right side. Using a 7.5mm stitch width, finished decorative seams will be about 1/2" wide. This double-binding method will be adapted for edges and decorative detail in later lessons.

1. To allow the extra fabric needed for wrapping a 1/4" seam allowance, before cutting out your garment or project, add an additional 1/2" to each edge that will be bound.

2. With right sides together, straight-stitch a seam using the seam allowance recommended on your pattern. (The seam allowance is usually 5/8" but may be 1/2" on home decorating projects.)

3. Press the seam allowances open and trim one allowance to a scant 1/4". From the right side, wrap the fabric securely around the trimmed allowance, forming a scant 1/4" fold. Press. (Fig. 3-15)

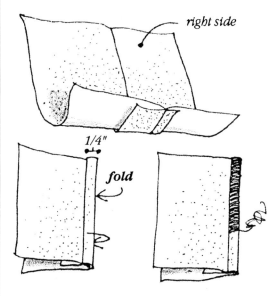

Fig. 3-15: *Make a double-bound seam by trimming the right seam allowance and wrapping the fabric around it. Serge-finish the fold.*

Special Tip: To minimize bulk on fabrics that do not ravel easily, try trimming the seam allowance to 1/8" before wrapping, then still press a scant 1/4" fold.

4. Use decorative thread in the upper and lower loopers and serger thread in the needle(s). Adjust for a wide, short, 3- or 3/4-thread stitch. Use a 7.5mm-wide stitch for the widest possible binding (or the use the widest stitch on your machine). For a stitch width narrower than 7.5mm, adjust the fold width so that the serged stitch will cover the entire fold. Test first.

5. Serge along the fold from the right side of the fabric, being careful not to cut the fold. The needle (the left needle on the 3/4-thread stitch) should be on the seamline. Adjust the tension so the overlocked stitches are tight against the fold.

6. Repeat steps 3 to 5 for the other seam allowance. When serging, make sure the needle stitches are right on or just inside the needleline of the first row of serging. (You will be serging in the direction opposite the first row of serging.) (Fig. 3-16)

7. Press the seam allowances open on the right side of the fabric. Use a press cloth, if necessary, to prevent melting the thread or leaving a shine.

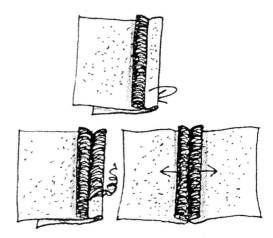

Fig. 3-16: Trim, wrap, and serge the other allowance, overlapping the needlelines. Press the allowances open.

Optional: If you will be securing the finished double-bound seam to the fabric, use decorative thread in the upper looper only. Use serger thread in the needle(s) and lower looper. Topstitch along each side of the binding. Or you may choose to use fusible thread in the lower looper when serge-finishing the folds, so you can fuse the binding to the fabric.

Double-piped seam

For this variation of the double-bound seam, follow the same procedure but use a narrow, balanced stitch on the 1/4" folds. The seam allowance will need to be trimmed to 1/4" (not narrower) so that it will catch in the narrower decorative serging and not pull out.

Note: With this technique, part of the fabric will show between the two sides of the binding. With a narrow, balanced stitch, the needlelines will not overlap. (Fig. 3-17) Alter stitch characteristics to vary the effect.

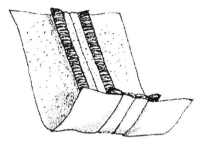

Fig. 3-17: The double-piped seam is a double-bound seam that is serged with a narrow, balanced stitch.

Project: Hobo Bag

A double-bound seam is featured on this easy-to-make, versatile bag. Vary the pattern size for different uses or to suit your personal style. (Fig. 3-18)

Fig. 3-18: This easy hobo bag features a double-bound seam.

Foot: Standard
Stitch: 3- or 3/4-thread overlock
Stitch length: Short
Stitch width: Widest
Thread: Contrasting color
    Needles(s): All-purpose or serger
    Upper looper: Woolly nylon
    Lower looper: Woolly nylon, all-purpose, serger, or fusible
Tension: Balanced
Needle(s): Size 11/75
Fabric: 3/4 yard 45"-wide water-repellent fabric or soft upholstery fabric
Notions: One pair 1" D-rings; 20" of 3/4"-wide *Velcro*; 1 yard of 1"-wide cotton or nylon strap

1. Cut two bag pieces using the

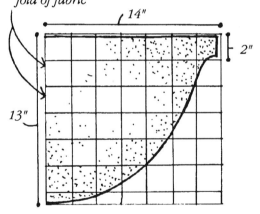

Fig. 3-19: The hobo bag pattern grid—each square is 2".

pattern grid. (Fig. 3-19)

2. Center one piece of *Velcro* on each wrong side of the top of the bag. Adjust the stitch length and width to the standard N setting. From the right side, serge the top of both bag pieces, catching the *Velcro* in the stitching.

 Special Tips: When serging with *Velcro*, do not use woolly nylon in the looper that carries stitches onto the *Velcro* piece. The woolly nylon's crimped fibers can catch on the *Velcro's* hooks and loops. Also test the stitch length first. You may need to lengthen the stitch when serging over *Velcro.*

3. Top-stitch the lower edge of the *Velcro* to each side of the bag.

4. With the right sides of the bag pieces together, straight-stitch around the lower edge with a 1/4" seam allowance. Trim one of the seam allowances to 1/8". Wrap the fabric around the trimmed seam allowance and press lightly (see Fig. 3-15, page 41).

5. Serge along the fold, being careful not to cut the fabric.

6. Repeat steps 4 and 5 for the other seam allowance.

7. Press open the seam allowances on the outside of the bag.

 Optional: To secure the seam allowances to the bag, use fusible thread in the lower looper when serge-finishing the fold. Then fuse the bound seam in place. Or top-stitch the bound seam allowances to the bag.

8. Serge across both narrow ends with fusible thread in the lower looper. Wrap each end around a D-ring. Fuse and top-stitch to secure the D-ring. (Fig. 3-20)

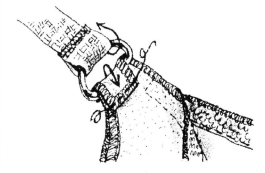

Fig. 3-20: *Secure the D-rings and straps by serge-finishing with fusible thread. Fuse them into position and top-stitch to reinforce them.*

9. Serge-finish each end of the strap with fusible thread in the lower looper. Insert each end of the strap through a D-ring. Fuse and top-stitch to secure.

Lesson 3. Flatlocked Seams

A flatlocked seam is always exposed on both sides of the fabric, so it can be used to add an interesting design detail. We most often see flatlocked seams on delicate lingerie and other garments on which sturdy seams are not essential. Although a flatlocked seam is relatively secure, it is not your best option for durability.

Perfecting flatlocking

A 3-thread overlock stitch is most commonly used for flatlocking with a *Hobbylock*. For this stitch, the needle thread tension is loosened so that the needle thread overlocks with the looper thread past the edge of the fabric. Because the needle thread is so loose, the seam can be pulled open until the stitches lie flat. (Fig. 3-21)

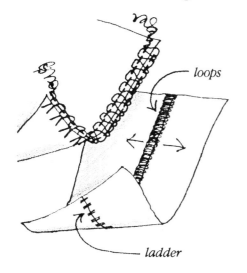

Fig. 3-21: *To flatlock, loosen the needle thread. Allow the stitches to hang off the edge. Pull the stitches flat after serging.*

The perfect flatlocked seam should be pulled completely flat. To do this, you must allow the stitches to hang off the edge as you serge. Feed the fabric under the presser foot slightly away from the knife. Your stitches will interlock beyond the edge, and you'll never have to worry about accidentally trimming your fabric. No amount of pressing will correct a flatlocked seam that cannot be pulled completely flat. Use the optional blindhem foot to guide the edge for an even flatlocked seam. Adjust the guide so the stitches will hang off the edge.

When flatlock seaming, you must trim the edges before serging because your fabric is fed through slightly away from the knives so the stitches will hang off the edge. If you are flatlock seaming a loosely woven fabric that will ravel and could pull out during use, serge-finish the cut edges first with a narrow, medium-length, balanced stitch using matching thread.

You may choose to have either the loops or the ladder side of a flatlock showing on the right side of your project (see Fig. 3-21). Both create a distinctive design detail. When flatlocking with decorative thread, keep in mind which part of your stitch will be exposed. Seaming with right sides together, the decorative thread must go through the eye of the *needle* if you want the ladder on the outside. But if the loops will be on the outside (seaming with wrong sides together), the decorative thread must be in the *upper looper*. For additional details on decorative flatlocking, see Lesson 25 (page 120).

Reinforced flatlock seaming

We often use this durable flatlock seaming method. First straight-stitch the seam on your sewing machine. You may choose to serge-finish the edges before stitching. Fold on the seamline with the wrong sides together if you want the loops to show. Fold with right sides together if you want to feature the ladder stitches. Using your widest stitch width, flatlock over the folded seam. Pull the stitching flat. If you have not serge-finished the seam allowances, trim them close to the stitching. (Fig. 3-22)

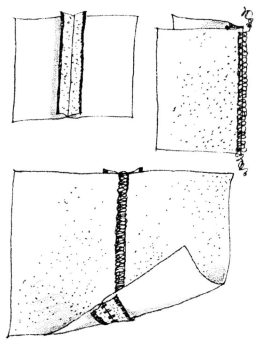

Fig. 3-22: For reinforced flatlocking, straight-stitch the seam. Fold the fabric and flatlock over the seamline.

O **Optional:** Eliminate the straight-stitching step by pressing the seam allowances back and placing them together. Flatlock over the folds and pull flat. This also makes a durable flatlocked seam.

Test each fabric or combination of fabrics before you flatlock. You may need to adjust tensions to accommodate the different thicknesses of your fabric. After flatlocking lace to tricot, for example, you may have to readjust your tensions before flatlock seaming two layers of tricot.

Project: Quick Slip

Whip up a pretty slip for any occasion with a length of tricot, two pieces of lace, and only three flatlocked seams. (Fig. 3-23)

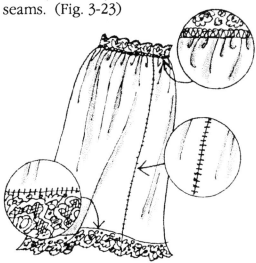

Fig. 3-23: Use flatlock seaming to make a quick and easy slip.

Foot: Standard
Stitch: 3-thread flatlock
Stitch length: Standard N to long
Stitch width: Standard N to widest
Thread: Matching color
  Needle: All-purpose, serger, or machine embroidery
  Upper looper: All-purpose, serger, or machine embroidery
  Lower looper: All-purpose, serger, or machine embroidery
Tension: Flatlock (needle thread loosened)
Needle: New, sharp size 11/75
Fabric: 1 length of nylon tricot, as long as you want your slip

Notions: Stretch lace (at least 3/4" wide, with one flat edge) to equal waist measurement; flat lace (with one flat edge) to equal slip bottom-edge measurement

1. Cut a fabric rectangle for the slip body. The length should equal the finished length desired minus the width of the flat lace. The width should be the hip measurement (measured 9" below the waist or at the widest part of the hip) plus 4". (Fig. 3-24)

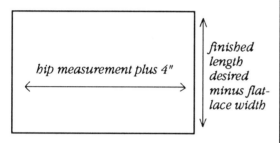

hip measurement plus 4"

finished length desired minus flat-lace width

Fig. 3-24: Cut nylon tricot for the slip.

2. You may want to serge-finish the upper and lower edges of the slip with a narrow, balanced stitch and matching thread to stabilize them and prevent them from rolling while flatlocking.

3. Adjust to a flatlock stitch. With right sides together, flatlock the flat lace to the bottom of the slip. Pull the seam flat.

4. Pull the stretch lace around your waist to a comfortable measurement (4" to 6" less than your waist measurement). Quartermark both the upper edge of the slip and the stretch lace. Match the markings. (The slip fabric is still flat, unseamed at the side.)

5. With the wrong sides together and the stretch lace on top, flatlock the stretch lace to the slip, stretching the lace to fit. Avoid hitting the pins.

6. Using the flatlock stitch and with right sides together, flatlock the side seam, matching the top and bottom laces. The less visible ladder stitches will show on the right side. Secure the seam ends by knotting the tails and trimming the remaining chain.

4. Decorative Edges

- **Lesson 4. Balanced Decorative Edges**
- **Lesson 5. Rolled Edges**
- **Lesson 6. Fishline Ruffles**
- **Lesson 7. Wire-shaped Edges**
- **Lesson 8. Reversible-edge Binding Stitch**
- **Lesson 9. Reversible Needle-wrap Stitch**

Finishing edges is a basic serger function. In fact, it is the only way some home-sewers use the serger. But edge-finishing can go way beyond the basics. By making simple tension changes and using decorative thread, you can transform edges into an ornamental element. When decoratively serge-finishing, it is important to consider how you will use the finished garment or project. If an edge will receive stress during use or wear, it must be stabilized in some way during construction or finishing. The stabilizing technique may be inconspicuous or decorative. Always test first with the thread and actual fabric you will be using.

When testing, look for stretching of the edges after they have been serge-finished. To prevent this, you may need to serge over a stabilizer such as elastic, cording, water-soluble stabilizer, or decorative trim. Or you may choose to serge over the fold of the fabric (see pages 58 and 70). Decorative serged bindings (featured in Chapter 5) will also stabilize an edge.

Check to see if the decorative serged stitch will pull away from the edge easily. (This occurs most often on chiffon and loosely woven or bias fabric.) If it does, you may need to lengthen or widen the stitch, serge the edge over water-soluble stabilizer, try another kind of decorative edge, or save the fabric for another project.

Lesson 4. Balanced Decorative Edges

As soon as you've mastered tension adjustment, you're ready to embellish your garments and other projects with simple ornamental edges. If just the top edge will be exposed, use decorative thread in the upper looper only. If both sides of the serging will show, use decorative thread in both loopers. (Fig. 4-1)

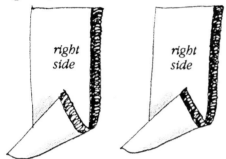

Fig. 4-1: *On a balanced edge, use decorative thread in the upper looper if only the right side will be exposed. When both sides will show, use it in both loopers.*

When decoratively serging curved edges, use a medium or narrow stitch width for easier handling and a neater stitch. If you plan to trim the edge while serge-finishing, clip away 2" of the seam allowance (along the serger cutting line) where you plan to begin and end the serging. (See the instructions for the hidden lapped serging technique, page 34.)

When serging outside corners, we usually simply serge off the fabric at each corner and then serge back onto the adjoining side. Most often, we secure the thread chain at each corner with seam sealant and clip the tail

when dry. This method eliminates any pretrimming if your project seam allowances are wider than the finished serged stitch.

Serge-scalloped edge

Your sewing machine and serger can team up to create some unusual ornamental effects. If your sewing machine has a variety of decorative stitches, try different ones in combination with a serged edge. Most sewing machines have a blindhem stitch that can be used to add a scalloped edge to your project. (Pfaff's newest sewing machine model has a scalloping stitch specifically for this.) In testing, we have found that this technique works best on a folded edge or two layers of light- or medium-weight fabric.

1. Serge-finish the edge. Use the same thread in both the upper and lower looper for ease in scalloping. To begin testing, adjust for a satin stitch length. The width of the stitch and the appearance of the scallops will vary with the weight of the fabric. Use your widest 3-thread stitch for medium- to heavy-weight fabrics and a narrower width for lightweight fabrics. (Fig. 4-2)

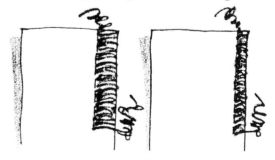

Fig. 4-2: *Use a wide stitch for medium- to heavy-weight fabrics. Use a narrower stitch for lightweight fabrics.*

2. Thread your sewing machine with thread matching the serged edge and adjust it for a blindhem stitch. Set the stitch width the same or slightly narrower than the serge-finished edge. With the serging to your left and the body of the fabric to your right, blindhem stitch the edge, allowing the zigzag of the stitch to go off the edge to form a scallop. You may have to tighten the needle tension slightly to make the edge more scalloped. Adjust the stitch length to test different sizes of scallops before finishing the garment edge. (Fig. 4-3)

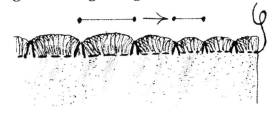

Fig. 4-3: *Test the length of a sewing machine blindhem stitch to create the desired size of scallop.*

S **Special Tip:** When using the blindhem stitch to scallop the edge of a project, you must feed the bulk of the fabric through the machine to the right of the needle. To avoid having to do this, use your machine's shell stitch (reversible blindhem stitch) or a scalloping stitch if you have one. These stitches will create the same effect, but the bulk of the fabric remains to the left of the needle.

Serge-corded edge

Serging over filler cord (such as one or more strands of heavier thread, string, or cording) creates a corded overlock that can be used to stabilize a serged edge and add durability. The size of the filler cord or the number of strands used will change the thickness of the serged edge. When decorative thread and a satin stitch length are also used, the serge-corded edge becomes an attractive ornamental feature.

When serging over filler cord, it is important to guide the cord carefully between the needle and the knife without stitching or cutting it, making sure that the upper looper goes cleanly over the top of the filler. For even application, place the filler under the back of the presser foot and over the front, against the left side of the knife guard. (Fig. 4-4)

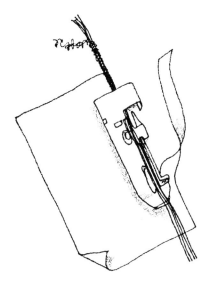

Fig. 4-4: *Serge over filler to create a corded edge.*

Begin serging over the filler cord by turning the hand wheel to make at least one stitch. Then begin serging at a slow speed to make sure that the cord is feeding correctly. Allow several inches of the filler to extend at the beginning and end of the serging.

To stabilize the edge, or when serge-cording around a curve, pull up on the filler to ease in the serged edge. Then knot securely. But remember, the rigid filler cord eliminates any stretch of the serged stitch.

To simplify the application of filler cord, use either the beading foot or ribbon foot (see page 12). (Fig. 4-5)

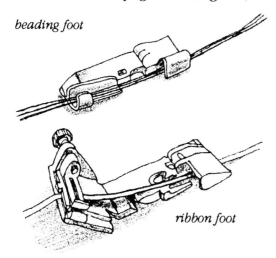

beading foot

ribbon foot

Fig. 4-5: *Use the beading foot or ribbon foot to simplify filler-cord application.*

Thread the **beading foot** according to the accompanying instructions (or those in the 797 manual). The filler feeds on top of the front guide and under the back guide. Either the right or left needle (needle C or B on the 797) may be used, depending on the size of the filler. Use the left needle (needle B) for larger, wider filler.

Thread the **ribbon foot** according to the instructions provided. The filler goes through the front guide, across the toe of the foot, and down under the back. You can use either needle for the ribbon application, but we usually prefer the left needle because of its wider stitch capability.

After attaching either the beading or ribbon foot and selecting the appropriate needle, place the filler through the guides and serge onto it for several inches before inserting the fabric. Hold the cord taut (and toward the right side of the needle, if necessary) as you serge over it.

After completing the application, lift the presser foot and draw the unattached filler tail under the foot to the left before chaining off. (Fig. 4-6)

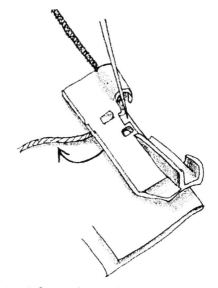

Fig. 4-6: *To chain off separately from the filler, lift the foot and draw the filler tail behind the needle.*

Serge-corded variations:

■ For an interesting ornamental effect, use monofilament nylon thread in the upper looper and a decorative filler.

■ For a thick, beefy serge-corded edge, use several strands of matching-color filler cord. Adjust for a narrow, balanced stitch and a short stitch length to replicate manufactured cording.

■ For a cording that gives with the fabric as well as stabilizes, use elastic cording or 1/8" transparent elastic for filler. The elastics are especially good for serged filler cording on sweatering, interlocks, and other knits.

Picot-braid edge

Serging along a finished edge with a picot-braid stitch creates a distinctive looped edging for a cuff or collar. When serged from the wrong side of the fabric, only a dainty row of picot stitches shows from the right side. When serged from the right side, the entire width of the stitch is visible. (Fig. 4-7)

1. Put a heavier decorative thread in the upper looper, monofilament nylon

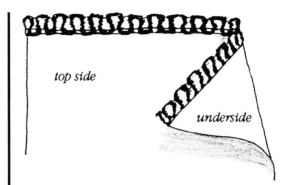

Fig. 4-7: Serge a picot-braid edge from either the right or wrong side with the needle just catching the fabric.

in the lower looper, and matching all-purpose or serger thread in the needle. Adjust for the widest, longest, 3-thread stitch with a balanced tension. For maximum width, try removing the decorative thread from the tension disc (see page 25).

2. Serge a few inches of braid before inserting the fabric. Stitch along the finished edge with the needle just catching the fabric.

3. Chain off a few inches of braid after completing the edge. Fold 1/2" of the chain ends to the underside and hand-tack to secure.

Project:
Sunburst T-shirt

Create a designer top by serge-decorating an inexpensive T-shirt. Have fun experimenting with different designs, thread types, and colors. (Fig. 4-8)

Fig. 4-8: *Decorate a T-shirt with narrow, balanced stitching. Ruffle the seamlines by stretching as you serge.*

Foot: Standard
Stitch: 3-thread
Stitch length: Short
Stitch width: Standard N with right needle
Thread: Contrasting color
   Needle: All-purpose or serger
   Upper looper: Woolly nylon
   Lower looper: Woolly nylon
Tension: Balanced
Needle: Size 11/75
Fabric: Oversized T-shirt
Notions: Beads (optional)

1. Purchase an inexpensive oversized T-shirt from a discount store. Most come in packages of three at additional savings, so you won't have to make a big investment for your testing.

2. With an air-erasable marking pen, draw a simple sunburst design on the front of the T-shirt. To do this, make six lines extending 6" to 7" from the neckline seam. Two lines will begin about 3/4" on either side of the center front. Two additional lines on each side begin at the neckline approximately 1-1/2" and 3" past the first lines. (Fig. 4-9)

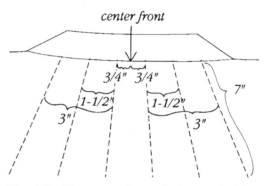

Fig. 4-9: *Draw a sunburst design on the T-shirt front with an air-soluble marker.*

3. With the wrong sides together, fold the T-shirt on each line. Starting at the neckline, serge over the folds to the end of the marked lines. Stretch the knit to ruffle the fabric as you serge, being careful not to cut the folds with the knives. Be sure to guide the folds so that the looper threads meet exactly at the edge. (If the fold is too wide, the thread will be stretched and will not have as much coverage.) Serge off the fabric at the end of each line and leave 4" to 6" of thread chain attached.

4. Using the same stitch adjustment and stretching as you sew, serge around the outer edge of the ribbed neckline. Start at one shoulder and end by serging approximately 1/2" over the beginning stitches, using the hidden lapped serging technique (page 34). Raise the presser foot and needle and pull the T-shirt away from the presser foot. Clip the thread ends.

5. Fold the ribbing to the inside along the neckline seamline. With the wrong sides together and the ribbing on top, begin serging over the fold, starting at one shoulder and stretching as you serge. (Fig. 4-10) Catch the

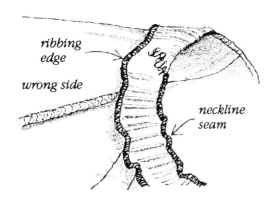

ribbing edge

wrong side

neckline seam

Fig. 4-10: *After ruffling the ribbing edge, fold the ribbing to the inside and serge over the neckline seam.*

ends of the sunburst lines in the stitching. Serge slowly when crossing the ends of the lines to allow maximum thread coverage. End by serging approximately 1/2" over the beginning stitches and pulling the top away from the presser foot as in step 4.

6. Repeat step 4 for the lower edge and sleeves. Start and end the lower-edge serging at one side seam. Start and end on the sleeves at the under-arm seam.

7. For a mock band effect at the lower edge, fold back and pin 3" with the wrong sides together. Serge over the fold, stretching as you sew. Repeat for the sleeve edges, folding back 1-1/2" before serge-finishing.

8. Tie on decorative beads to the end of each sunburst thread chain if desired.

Lesson 5.
Rolled Edges

The narrow rolled edge (or hem) makes a wonderful finish for most light- and medium-weight fabrics on any project from napkins to expensive dresses. With some adjustments, you also may be able to use a rolled edge on heavier fabrics. A rolled-edge finish may be either decorative or inconspicuous, depending upon the thread used. One of the original selling points of the home serger was its ability to do a rolled edge more neatly, quickly, and easily than on a sewing machine.

Consult your manual for instructions on converting to a rolled hem. You will need to use the right needle and change to the rolled-hem foot.

The only visible thread in a correctly adjusted 3-thread rolled edge is the upper looper thread. (Fig. 4-11)

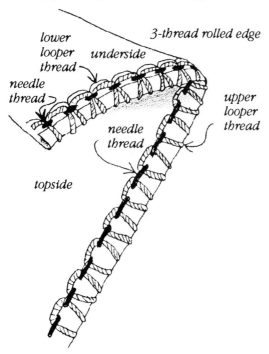

Fig. 4-11: *The upper looper thread wraps the edge. The lower looper and needle threads are barely visible.*

When the tension is adjusted properly, the upper looper thread is pulled entirely around the edge of the fabric from needleline to needleline. The lower looper thread is tightened and forms a line that is almost straight. Both the lower looper and needle threads can barely be seen.

For a rolled edge, you will need only one spool or cone of decorative thread. With some decorative threads (and on certain fabrics), you may find it impossible to wrap the upper looper thread entirely around to the back using tension adjustment alone. A classic example is with slick rayon thread. Use woolly nylon or monofilament nylon thread in the lower looper. The added strength of the nylon will help roll the edge completely. With monofilament nylon in the lower looper, loosen the tension before starting to serge. If the tension is too tight, the monofilament thread may snap. Because it is practically invisible, monofilament is more difficult to rethread.

To form a rolled-edge stitch, the fabric must roll completely around the needlelike stitch finger. If your serger doesn't cut the seam allowance portion wide enough to wrap around the stitch finger, short threads may poke out through the stitching. (Fig. 4-12)

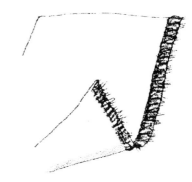

Fig. 4-12: *Threads may poke through the stitching on a rolled edge if the seam allowance is not wide enough to wrap to the underside or if the stitch is too long.*

Try these solutions to eliminate the problem:

1. Adjust your machine for a wider stitch. We find it easiest to start serging a rolled edge with the standard N stitch width, then gradually increase or narrow it as we test.

2. Shorten the stitch length to completely cover the edge with serged stitches.

3. Use monofilament or woolly nylon thread in the lower looper.

4. Place a strip of water-soluble stabilizer over the fabric edge before rolling it. Tear away the excess stabilizer after serging.

5. Press 1/4" to the wrong side and serge the rolled edge over the fold (see Serge-a-fold, page 58).

 Note: If threads extend beyond the stitching on the underside (rather than poking out to the side), adjust the knife by narrowing the bite. (Fig. 4-13)

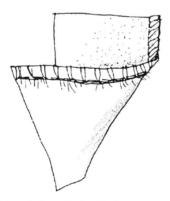

Fig. 4-13: Adjust the knife for a narrower bite if threads extend beyond the stitching on the underside.

Wiry fibers in your fabric or serging on the crosswise grain may also cause threads to poke through, but making the adjustments listed will usually correct the problem.

When serging loosely woven or lightweight fabrics, the rolled edge may pull away from the fabric. This occurs most often when serging with a short stitch length. If this happens, lengthen the stitch slightly. You may have to widen the bite, too. The grainline of the fabric may also be a factor when the edge separates from the fabric. Test-serge on both the lengthwise and crosswise grains, as well as on the bias.

Lettucing

Lettucing the edge is a finish used only on fabric that will stretch, such as knits and bias wovens. To make a ruffled lettuce edge, you must stretch while serging, using a very short (satin) stitch length. (Fig. 4-14) Be

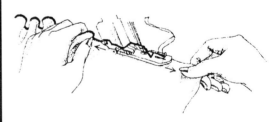

Fig. 4-14: Lettuce the edge of a stretch or bias fabric by stretching while serging.

careful not to bend the needle while stretching the fabric. If you have differential feed, adjust it to 0.5 to help with the stretching.

Because the fabric is stretched while serging, you may need to widen the bite, if possible, to allow enough fabric to roll over the stitch finger.

Double rolled edge

Two rows of rolled edge serged directly next to each other make an unusual ornamental detail that is also very durable. Use two contrasting thread colors, or try two different thread types for a heightened effect.

1. Serge the wrong side of one edge of the fabric with a satin rolled edge, leaving several inches of thread chain. (Fig. 4-15) Woolly nylon or a heavier rayon will provide the maximum thread coverage.

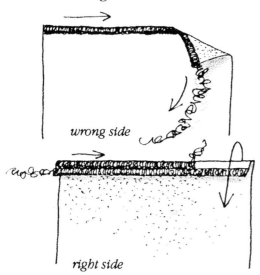

Fig. 4-15: Create a double rolled edge by serging one row from the wrong side. Then fold the stitching to the right side and serge the second row on the fold.

2. Rethread the upper looper with a contrasting thread.

3. With right sides together, refold the fabric next to the first rolled edge, leaving just enough width for another rolled-edge seam allowance.

4. Holding the thread chain to prevent jamming, serge a second rolled edge over the fold with the needle right next to the needleline of the original stitching. For serging accuracy, line up the first rolled edge with the raised ridge on top of the rolled-edge presser foot. (Fig. 4-16) You will be serging in the opposite direction from the first serging.

5. Carefully press the double rolled edge flat.

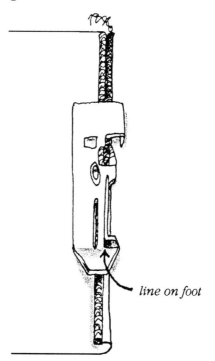

line on foot

Fig. 4-16: Use the ridge on the presser foot as a guide for the second row of the double rolled edge.

Scalloped rolled edge

The scalloped rolled edge is similar to the scalloped edge made using balanced stitching (page 49). This edge-finish is seen on the finest ready-to-wear lingerie. If you are using a scalloped rolled edge on nylon tricot, remember that tricot rolls to the right side. For the nicest rolled edge and the least frustration, serge the rolled edge from the wrong side.

Serge-a-fold

The rolled edge is a durable edge in itself. But if you prefer more body on the edge, are having trouble with threads poking through the stitching, or feel the serged edge may pull off a loosely woven fabric, press the edge 1/4" to the wrong side and serge the rolled edge over the fold. (Fig. 4-17) On the wrong side, trim the raw edge right next to the serging.

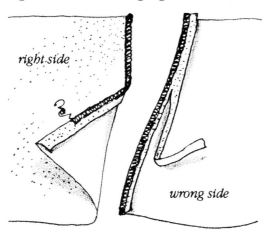

right side

wrong side

Fig. 4-17: *For durability and to eliminate threads poking through the stitching, serge over a folded edge. Trim the excess seam allowance on the wrong side.*

If the edge will be visible from both the top and underside, straight-stitch right next to the fold and trim the raw edge close to the stitching before applying the rolled edge.

For even more durability, combine serging on the fold with scalloped edging. If you are using a scalloped rolled edge on a single knit, the decorative stitch has a tendency to roll to the right side. To prevent this and add more body, serge-finish the edge with a narrow, balanced stitch, press 1/4" to the wrong side, and serge over the fold. Finish with the blindhem stitch to create scallops.

Picot rolled edge

This variation of the rolled edge is most often used on soft fabric such as tricot. It finishes the edges of lingerie garments and silky scarves beautifully. To make an attractive picot edge, simply alter a rolled-edge stitch (see page 54) for a long stitch length and tighten the upper looper tension slightly. (Fig. 4-18)

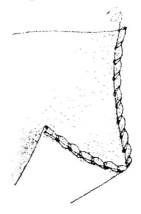

Fig. 4-18: *Serge a picot rolled edge by lengthening and slightly tightening the upper looper of a rolled-edge stitch.*

Tuck-and-roll

This decorative edge is made using a 3/4-thread stitch and two needles with the rolled-edge tension adjustments. It can be used on garments or other projects—anywhere you'd consider using a basic rolled edge. (Fig. 4-19)

Fig. 4-19: The tuck-and-roll edge is created by serging a rolled edge with a 3/4-thread stitch.

1. Adjust for a rolled-edge stitch (see page 54), but use both needles and either the standard or beading presser foot. Tighten the upper looper tension slightly.

 Note: The rolled-edge foot will not work for this technique.

2. Using a satin stitch length, serge the edge. A tuck will form to the right of both needles. You may want to use woolly nylon or monofilament nylon thread in the lower looper to pull the decorative thread completely around the rolled fabric on the edge.

3. For a wider tuck-and-roll, use a wide stitch with the same tension adjustments. The tuck will not be as pronounced in the wider stitch.

Project: Christmas Tree Bags

These cute little Christmas tree bags are quick to make for gifts or decorating. The rolled-edge stitch seams and finishes the bags in one step, leaving attractive thread chains for the handles. (Fig. 4-20)

Fig. 4-20: Stow tiny gifts, candies, or holiday ornaments in these simple little tree bags. The rolled-edge seams and handles are serged all in one.

Foot: Rolled edge
Stitch: 3-thread
Stitch length: Short
Stitch width: Standard N with right
    needle
Thread: Contrasting color
    Needle: All-purpose or serger
    Upper looper: Heavier metallic
        thread, like Candlelight
    Lower looper: Monofilament
        nylon
Tension: Rolled edge
Needle: Size 11/75
Fabric: Scraps of Christmas fabric
Notions: Four bells for each bag

1. Cut two 2-1/2" by 3" rectangles for each bag. With a cup or jar lid, round the two lower corners of each rectangle. (Fig. 4-21)

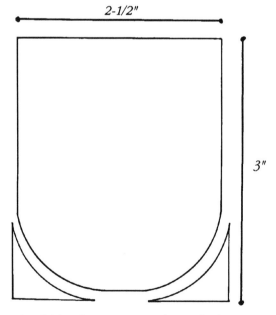

Fig. 4-21: Cut two rectangles 2-1/2" by 3". Round the lower corners.

2. Cut a side and bottom strip 8" long by 1-1/2" wide for each bag.

3. On the top of each rectangle and the short end of each strip, fold 1/4" to the wrong side and serge over the fold. Trim the fabric close to the stitching on the wrong side.

4. Serge the strip around the sides and bottom of one rectangle, with wrong sides together and the rectangle on the top. (Fig. 4-22) Leave about 6" of thread chain on each end. Hold the thread chain taut to prevent

Fig. 4-22: Leaving a long thread chain, serge the side strip to the bag piece. Pull the strip around to meet curved edges.

jamming. When serging the curves, pull them around to meet the straight edge of the strip.

5. Repeat step 4 for the other rectangle.

6. Tie a bell to the end of each chain and knot the four chains together about 2" from the bells (see Fig. 4-20).

Lesson 6.
Fishline Ruffles

The beautiful fishline ruffle, like its ready-to-wear forerunner, is most often seen on special-occasion garments and floral-like embellishments. Fishline is applied to the edge of the fabric similarly to filler cord, using a short- to medium-length, rolled-edge stitch. (Fig. 4-23)

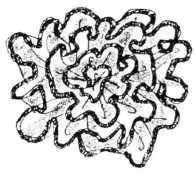

Fig. 4-23: Fishline ruffles add unusual ornamental effects.

Fishline is available at most sporting goods, discount, and drug stores in weights varying from 12 lb. to 40 lb. The lighter weight is better for lightweight fabrics like tulle and netting. Use a medium weight (25 lb.) for fabrics such as satin and taffeta. Also use a heavier fishline if you are serging over two layers of fabric or if you want extra body. If you are edge-finishing a lightweight or sheer fabric such as tulle, be sure to use clear fishline.

Serging on bias fabric creates the prettiest ruffles, but on a loosely woven fabric the stitching may pull off. As an alternative, cut the fabric on the lengthwise grain.

While serging, it is important to guide accurately and **serge slowly**. If you accidentally cut the fishline while serging over it, you will need to rework part of your project.

For the tightest fishline edge, use the rolled-edge foot. Place the fishline under the back of the presser foot and hold it against the right side of the foot's needle guard to guide it between the guard and the knife, as shown. (Fig. 4-24)

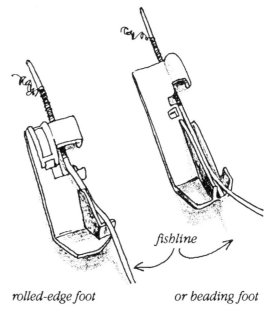

fishline

rolled-edge foot   *or beading foot*

Fig. 4-24: For fishline ruffles, serge over fishline, then stretch after serging.

On the 786, 784, and 783, this technique works beautifully, guiding the fishline under the fabric. With the rolled-edge foot on the 797, however, the fishline is more difficult to control when applying it this way. An easy alternative is to use the beading foot, as you would for serging over filler cord (page 50), holding the fishline against the right side of the guide.

When serging over fishline, leave a long tail at the beginning and end of the serging (about half the ruffle length). First serge over the fishline for several inches, then place the fabric underneath. Do not stretch while serging. After serging, stretch for the amount of ruffling or flouncing desired.

Project: Ruffled Doily

A fishline ruffle adorns the edge of this charming doily. Use it under a dining table centerpiece or to add a decorative touch on a small table or chest. (Fig. 4-25)

Fig. 4-25: *Fishline ruffles edge a centerpiece doily.*

Foot: Standard for serge-finishing; rolled edge or beading for ruffle
Stitch: 3-thread for serge-finishing; rolled edge for ruffle
Stitch length: Standard N for serge-finishing; short for rolled edge
Stitch width: Widest for serge-finishing; standard N with right needle for rolled edge
Thread: Matching color
 Needle: All-purpose or serger
 Upper looper: All-purpose or serger for serge-finishing; rayon for rolled edge
 Lower looper: All-purpose or serger for serge-finishing; monofilament nylon for rolled edge
Tension: Balanced for serge-finishing; rolled edge for ruffle
Needle: Size 11/75
Fabric: 1/4 yard polyester/cotton eyelet; 1 yard matching woven cotton
Notions: 4 yards clear 30-lb. fishline; contrasting-color button hole twist or crochet thread for gathering

1. Cut a 9" circle from the eyelet, using a plate or large lid as a pattern. Serge-finish the edge.

2. Cut 4"-wide bias strips from the matching woven cotton and serge-seam them to make 2 yards of ruffled trim.

3. Change to the rolled-edge or beading foot. With rayon thread in the upper looper and monofilament nylon thread in the lower looper, serge-finish one long edge of the trim with a rolled edge.

4. Using the fishline ruffle techniques on page 61, serge over approximately 6" of fishline before inserting the fabric under the presser foot. Serge-finish the second long trim edge with the fishline, leaving approximately 6" of fishline at the end. After serging, stretch the fishline edge to ruffle.

5. Gather the ruffle on the edge opposite the fishline, 3/8" from the rolled edge. Zigzag over a strand of buttonhole twist or crochet thread, being careful not catch the heavier thread in the stitching. Position the left side of the presser foot next to the rolled edge as a guide.

6. Gather the trim to fit the outer serge-finished edge of the eyelet. Straight-stitch the two short ends of the trim to form a circle. Use a short stitch length and back-stitch to secure the fishline.

7. Distribute the gathers evenly and top-stitch the trim to the eyelet circle by zigzagging over the gathering line. Be careful not to catch the heavier gathering thread in the stitching. Remove the gathering thread to complete the doily.

Lesson 7.
Wire-shaped Edges

Much like fishline, fine wire can be used to shape serged edges. Unlike fishline, however, it is rigid and can be formed into almost any shape. (Fig. 4-26)

Fig. 4-26: Fine wire shapes a delicate rolled edge.

Fine wire is available in any craft store. We first used lightweight floral wire to shape edges of serged flowers and for serged-wire ornaments. Because most floral wire is precut to 18" lengths, we also now use fine beading wire, which comes on spools and in a variety of weights and colors.

When you serge a wire-shaped edge, it is essential that you guide the wire carefully and **serge slowly** (use the half-speed setting on the foot pedal). If you serge too fast, you may hit the wire with a needle, which could throw your serger out of alignment. Wire-shaped projects are for more experienced serger users, and even they need to be very careful.

The easiest method of applying a wire-shaped edge is to use the beading foot (see page 12). The foot

guides the wire safely between the
needle and knife. (Fig. 4-27)

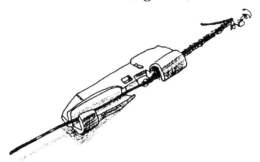

Fig. 4-27: *Serging over fine wire is easy using the beading foot.*

If you do not have a beading foot, use the rolled-edge foot. Guide the wire under the back of the presser foot and carefully between the foot and the knife in the front, holding it away from the knife.

When serging over wire, leave at least a 1" tail at both ends for securing. Begin by serging over the wire for at least one additional inch. Pull gently on the thread chain and the wire tail to guide the serging smoothly. Then raise the presser foot and position the fabric under the foot and wire. Serge slowly. After some fabric clears the back of the presser foot, bend the wire back over the fabric to anchor it during the remainder of the serging. (Fig. 4-28)

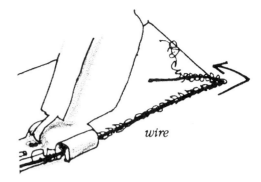

Fig. 4-28: *Start serging over the wire, then insert the fabric. Bend the wire back over the fabric to anchor.*

Project: Wind Twister

This colorful outdoor ornament is shaped by rolled-edge serging over wire on one long edge. It twists merrily as the breezes blow. (Fig. 4-29)

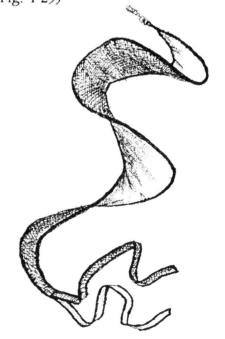

Fig. 4-29: *Wind twister with wire-shaped edges.*

Foot: Rolled edge; beading foot for wire application
Stitch: 3-thread
Stitch length: Short
Stitch width: Standard N with right needle
Thread: Coordinating color
  Needle: All-purpose or serger
  Upper looper: Woolly nylon
  Lower looper: Woolly nylon
Tension: Rolled edge
Needle: Size 11/75
Fabric: 1/2 yard each of two colors 45"-wide, water-repellent nylon, such as taffeta or *Ripstop*
Notions: 20-gauge beading wire (found in craft stores); one barrel swivel (from fishing supply stores)

1. Using the pattern grid (Fig. 4-30), cut one twister and one 18" by 2" strip from each piece of nylon.

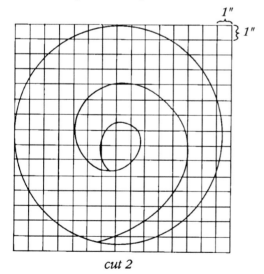

cut 2

Fig. 4-30: *Pattern grid for wind twister.*

2. Adjust for a rolled edge. Serge-finish the two long sides and one short end of each strip.

3. Serge the matching color strip to the narrow end of each nylon twister piece, right sides together.

4. Place the twister pieces wrong sides together and serge-finish the inner edge of the circle.

5. Serge over 4" to 5" of wire, then insert the top of the twister and serge the wire to the outer edge of the twister circle, stopping approximately 1" past the tail seamline. Then serge off the fabric but continue serging over the wire for another 6". Raise the presser foot and the needle, pull the wire back and away from the presser foot, and serge off. Cut the wire, leaving 12" past the end of the serging.

6. Smooth the fabric over the wire, beginning at the upper edge. Twist the lower end of the wire back on itself to secure, then clip away the excess wire. Attach the barrel swivel to the serged wire at the top of the twister.

7. Place the twister on a flat surface and flatten the wire into the original circle shape. Hang the twister from the barrel swivel.

Lesson 8. Reversible-edge Binding Stitch

The upper looper thread wraps the fabric edge to form the reversible-edge binding stitch. Similar to the rolled-edge stitch, reversible-edge binding is used for heavier fabrics on which the edges do not roll under. Single-layer coats and blanket edges are common applications. Use heavier thread in the upper looper for a more durable edge.

For reversible-edge binding, use the standard presser foot and the standard N stitch width with the right needle only. Loosen the upper looper tension and tighten the lower looper tension. The thread should completely wrap the edge and look the same on both the upper and under side. (Fig. 4-31) If the thread does not wrap completely after loosening the tension, take the thread entirely

out of the tension disc (see page 25). Narrowing the stitch width will also help wrap the edge.

 Special Tip: If tension adjustments give a less-than-perfect stitch, switch to woolly nylon in the lower looper. This strong thread often helps to wrap the stitch completely.

The reversible-edge binding stitch is a simple but decorative edge finish, ideal for place mats, potholders, or cozies made from quilted fabrics. Before serging the edge of quilted fabric, compress the thickness by zigzagging over the area to be serged, using a long, wide stitch. Then serge directly over the zigzagging.

Project: Wool Lap Robe

The top of this 48" by 72" lap robe can be crazy-quilted from serged-together wool scraps. Or choose a soft wool yardage to complement your decor. (Fig. 4-32)

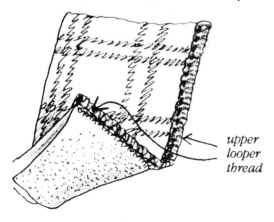

upper looper thread

Fig. 4-31: *For reversible-edge binding, loosen the upper looper and tighten the lower looper. The upper looper thread should completely wrap the edge.*

Fig. 4-32: *Wool lap robe combines wool scraps with a flannel backing. The edge is finished with a reversible-edge binding stitch.*

Foot: Standard

Stitch: 3-thread for decorative edge; 3- or 3/4-thread for serging patchwork

Stitch length: Short for binding; standard N for serging patchwork

Stitch width: Standard N (or narrower) for binding; wide for serging patchwork

Thread: Contrasting or matching color

Needle(s): All-purpose or serger

Upper looper: Acrylic or cotton crochet thread for binding; serger thread for patchwork

Lower looper: All-purpose, serger, or woolly nylon

Tension: Tightened lower looper and loosened upper looper for the binding; balanced for serging patchwork

Needle(s): Size 14/90

Fabric: Wool scraps to make a 48" by 72" piece (or 2 yards of 54" or wider soft wool or acrylic) for the robe top; 2 yards of 54" or wider flannel for the backing

1. If you are using wool scraps, serge them together in any pattern to construct a piece measuring 48" by 72". (Fig. 4-33) Or cut the lap robe top from soft wool or acrylic to the same measurement. Cut a flannel backing piece measuring 48" by 72".

2. Adjust for a reversible-edge binding stitch.

3. With the wrong sides of the top and the backing together, serge both lengthwise edges. Then serge the crosswise edges.

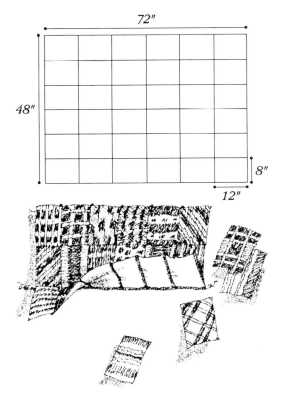

Fig. 4-33: Serge together wool scraps for top of lap robe.

4. Secure the thread chain on each corner by threading it back through the binding stitch using a darning needle or a loop turner.

Lesson 9. Reversible Needle-wrap Stitch

Another decorative reversible stitch is the needle wrap, also called the blanket stitch. In this crochet-like edging, the needle thread wraps to the edge on both sides of the fabric, so the decorative thread used must be able to be threaded through the needle. The looper threads interlock at the edge of the fabric. (Fig. 4-34)

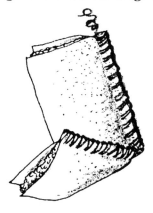

Fig. 4-34: The reversible needle-wrap stitch makes a crochet-like edging. It is formed when the needle tension is loosened and the looper tension is tightened.

Use the needle-wrap stitch as a decorative detail on an already-finished edge (such as a faced neckline or a hem foldline), or use it to finish edges on firmly woven fabric.

Using the standard presser foot, adjust for a short 3-thread overlock stitch with a standard N or narrower stitch width and the right needle. Loosen the needle tension and tighten the upper and lower looper tensions so the threads interlock on the edge. If the threads do not overlock exactly at the edge, adjust them with your tweezers.

If you cannot loosen the needle thread entirely to the edge by making a tension adjustment, use a narrower

stitch width. Also try woolly nylon in the loopers to help perfect this decorative stitch, or remove the needle thread from the tension guides.

The look of a crocheted edge is most easily created by using a long stitch length for the needle-wrap stitch. It also works best with the heaviest possible thread that can fit through the needle eye.

Project: Quick Potholder

Whip up a batch of simple washable potholders with reversible needle-wrap edging. You will always have clean ones on hand, and they're great for gifts, too. (Fig. 4-35)

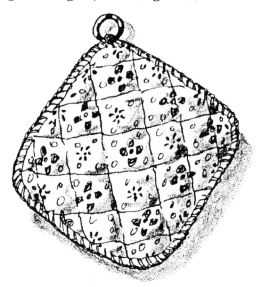

Fig. 4-35: Speedy serged potholders are made by sandwiching insulating material between quilted fabric, then needle-wrapping the edges.

Foot: Standard
Stitch: 3-thread
Stitch length: Standard N
Stitch width: Standard N or nar-
    rower with right needle
Thread: Contrasting color
    Needle: Buttonhole twist
    Upper looper: Woolly nylon
    Lower looper: Woolly nylon
Tension: Loosened needle tension
    and tightened looper tensions
Needle: Size 11/75 or 14/90
Fabric: 1/4 yard single-faced
    quilted; 1/4 yard insulating mate-
    rial, like *Thinsulate* or a *Teflon*
    ironing-board cover

1. Cut two 8" by 8" squares of the quilted fabric and one of the insulating fabric for each potholder.

2. Layer the quilted fabric with wrong sides together and sandwich the insulating fabric in between.

3. Round the corners using a small bowl or lid as a guide.

4. Zigzag around the edges to compress the quilted fabric.

5. Adjust your serger for a reversible needle-wrap stitch. Test on project scraps following the instructions on page 67.

6. Starting in the middle of one straight side, serge around the edges using the needle-wrap stitch and just skimming the edges with the knives. Overlap the beginning stitching for about 1/2". Then raise the presser foot and needle and pull the potholder away from the foot. Dab the ends with seam sealant and clip the tails when dry.

7. After serging, you may have to pull the needle thread with tweezers, especially on the corners, so the overlocking looper thread is right on the edge.

8. Hand-tack a round plastic curtain loop to one corner if desired.

5. Decorative Trims, Braids, and Bindings

- **Lesson 10. Serged-fold Self Braid**
- **Lesson 11. Quick-fused Self-Braid**
- **Lesson 12. Serged Self-Binding**
- **Lesson 13. Double-bound Edge**
- **Lesson 14. Serged Piping**
- **Lesson 15. Serged Binding**
- **Lesson 16. Serge-piped Binding**
- **Lesson 17. Double Rolled-edge Braid and Binding**
- **Lesson 18. Elasticized Trims and Binding**
- **Lesson 19. Tear-away Braid**
- **Lesson 20. Puffed Serged Braid**
- **Lesson 21. Serged Picot Braid**
- **Lesson 22. Serged Couching Braid**

Decorative trims and bindings can be serged directly onto the edge of your fabric, creating self-binding for craft and home decoration projects as well as for garments from sporty to elegant. Trims and bindings can also be made using a separate strip of fabric that is then attached to your garment or project.

Many of the edge finishes you learned in Chapter 4 can be used separately or in combination to make a wide variety of ornamental trims and bindings. In addition to adding a unique decorative element, trims and bindings also help finish and stabilize project edges.

When applying edge-finishing or self-binding directly to your fabric, always test first for stretching. If the area you will be finishing (especially a bias-woven or a cross-grain knit edge) stretches during the application, serge your trim onto a strip of fabric and bind the edge instead.

Lesson 10. Serged-fold Self-Braid

Many pretty edge finishes are not as stable as we may need for a particular project or fabric. In many cases, a neckline that is finished single-layer will stretch out. Or a single-layer sleeve edge on a loosely woven fabric may not hold up. With serged-fold self-braid, the fabric edge is folded for more durability before serge-finishing. Heavy threads serged on the fold of heavy fabric can look similar to an actual braid trim. Lighter-weight threads serged on the fold of fine fabric give a more delicate, but stable, finish.

1. Press 1/2" to the wrong side. Turning less than a 1/2" allowance may make it more difficult to keep a uniform edge.

2. Top-stitch 1/8" from the fold with a long stitch length. If your finished project edge will be visible from both sides, trim the allowance close to the top-stitching.

3. Put decorative thread in the upper looper and, if the underside will be visible, also use decorative thread in the lower looper. If only the right side will be exposed, you may use all-purpose or serger thread in the lower looper as well as in the needle.

4. Place the folded edge next to the knife and serge with a short, narrow, and balanced 3-thread stitch. Guide carefully, or use a blindhem foot to prevent cutting the fold (see page 11).

 Special Tips: If you are using heavy thread, lengthen the stitch to prevent jamming when you begin to serge. Too much thread coverage may also cause stretching or ruffling of the edge. If your model has differential feed, set it on 1.5 to ease in the edge (especially on bias edges). Always test first on project fabric scraps.

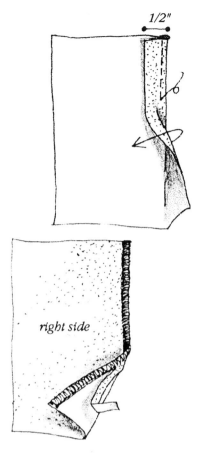

Fig. 5-1: *Create serged-fold self-braid by pressing 1/2" to the wrong side and serge-finishing the fold. Trim the allowance to the stitching before serging if the wrong side will be visible; do this after serging if it will not.*

5. If you haven't previously trimmed the excess allowance, do so now. Use sharp embroidery or appliqué scissors and trim close to the serging. (Fig. 5-1)

To vary the serged-fold edge, adjust for a rolled-edge stitch (page 54) or a reversible-edge binding stitch (page 66).

For a more pronounced serged-fold self-braid, serge over filler cord as discussed in Lesson 4 (page 50). (Fig. 5-2) For bias and curved areas, pull on the filler to ease the serged edge.

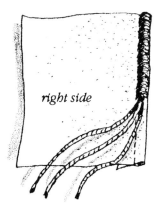

Fig. 5-2: Serge over filler threads for more pronounced braid.

Project: Lace-edged Handkerchief

Glossy serged-fold self-braid and dainty lace finish the edge of this feminine handkerchief. Make four out of only one-third yard of fabric. (Fig. 5-3)

Fig. 5-3: Lace-edged handkerchief with serged-fold braid edging.

Foot: Standard or blindhem
Stitch: 3-thread
Stitch length: Short
Stitch width: Standard N with right needle
Thread: Matching color
  Needle: All-purpose or serger
  Upper looper: Rayon
  Lower looper: All-purpose or serger
Tension: Balanced
Needle: Size 11/75
Fabric: 1/3 yard organdy or fine batiste
Notions: 1-1/4 yard 1/2"- to 1"-wide flat scalloped lace (with one straight edge) for each handkerchief

1. Cut an 11" by 11" square of fabric.

2. On two opposite edges, press 1/2" to the wrong side.

3. Top-stitch 1/8" from the fold. Trim the allowance close to the stitching.

4. Serge-finish both folds with a short, standard N-width, balanced 3-thread stitch.

 Optional: Use the blindhem foot as a guide for even stitching. Use the right needle only.

5. Repeat steps 2, 3, and 4 for both remaining edges.

6. Fold 1/2" of the lace to the wrong side at one end. Beginning 1" from one corner, lap the serge-finished handkerchief edge over the straight edge of the lace with the right sides up. Top-stitch along the edge of the serged-fold self-braid, close to the needleline, catching the lace in the stitching.

7. Fold the lace at each corner to miter. When you reach the beginning of the lace trim, fold 1/2" to the right side and lap it 1/2" under the beginning lace before completing the top-stitching. (Fig. 5-4)

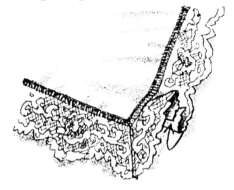

Fig. 5-4: Lap the folded ends of the lace to finish the handkerchief.

Lesson 11. Quick-fused Self-Braid

Create another simple self-trim by serge-finishing garment or project edges from the wrong side using fusible thread in the lower looper. Then fold the serged edge to the right side and fuse it into position.

The width of the finish can be varied by pressing additional fabric plus the serged edge to the right side. For this variation, the wrong side of the fabric will show as part of the braid. Therefore, the wrong side of the fabric must match or intentionally contrast with the right side.

1. Thread your serger with decorative thread in the upper looper, fusible thread in the lower looper, and all-purpose or serger thread in the needle.

2. From the wrong side, serge-finish the edge with a short, wide, and balanced 3-thread stitch.

3. Press the edge to the right side and fuse it in place. If you are pressing more than the width of the serged stitch to the right side, cut out the project with a corresponding allowance for the extra fabric. (Fig. 5-5)

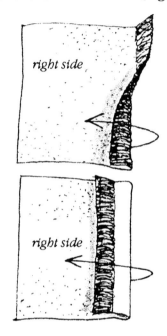

Fig. 5-5: For quick-fused self-braid, decoratively finish the edge from the wrong side with fusible thread in the lower looper. Press the stitching to the right side and fuse it next to the edge or further over.

For a heavier braid, add a wide decorative finish over a narrow self-braid.

1. Serge-finish the edge from the wrong side with a narrow, medium-length, and balanced 3-thread stitch with fusible thread in the lower looper.

2. Fold the stitched edge to the right side and fuse to secure.

3. Change to decorative thread in the lower looper and adjust your serger for a wide satin stitch. Serge over the narrow fused edge. (Fig. 5-6)

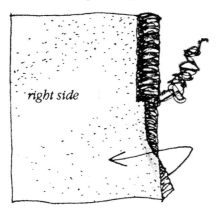

right side

Fig. 5-6: *For heavier braid, make a narrow quick-fused self-braid. Then serge over it with decorative thread and a wide stitch.*

Project: Quickie Shoe Bags

The casing for these fast and easy shoe bags is decoratively finished with quick-fused self-braid. The flannel fabric serves a double purpose: It keeps the shoes clean and buffs them at the same time—great for a business traveler. (Fig. 5-7)

Fig. 5-7: *Flannel shoe bags feature an easy quick-fused self-braid casing.*

Foot: Standard
Stitch: 3-thread
Stitch length: Short for decorative; standard N for serge-finishing
Stitch width: Widest
Thread: Contrasting color for decorative; matching for serge-finishing
Needle: All-purpose or serger
Upper looper: Crochet thread for decorative; all-purpose or serger for serge-finishing
Lower looper: Fusible thread for decorative; all-purpose or serger for serge-finishing
Tension: Balanced
Needle: Size 11/75
Fabric: 1/2 yard cotton flannel
Notions: One pair 27" shoelaces

1. For a pair of shoe bags, cut two 15" by 17" rectangles from the flannel.

2. From the wrong side, decoratively serge-finish one 15" edge on each piece for the upper casings (using crochet thread in the upper looper and fusible thread in the lower looper).

3. Rethread the upper and lower loopers with all-purpose or serger thread. Serge-finish the remaining three sides of both pieces.

4. Fold each bag lengthwise, right sides together, and straight-stitch the lower edge with a 1/4" seam allowance. Pivot at the corner and continue straight-stitching the side seam, ending 1" from the top edge. Back-stitch to secure the stitching. (Fig. 5-8)

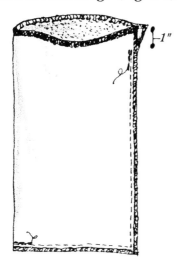

Fig. 5-8: Straight-stitch the bottom and side of the bag, leaving 1" unstitched at the top edge.

5. On each bag, fold the decoratively serged edge 1" to the right side and carefully press to fuse the casing edge. Top-stitch over the serged needleline to secure. Insert a shoelace into the casing and draw the bag closed.

Lesson 12. Serged Self-Binding

A simple self-binding technique uses part of the fabric to bind the edge. It is stable as well as decorative and can be a good option for a neckline facing or a center-front band. Self-binding is most often used on straight edges and stable woven fabrics, but it can be applied to curved areas on knit fabrics as well.

The width of the finished binding is determined by the width of the serged stitch. Use the widest stitch possible on your serger. The 7.5mm stitch (available on most *Hobbylock* models) with heavy-weight decorative thread makes the beefiest self-bound edge.

To make serged self-binding, add a 7/8" binding allowance to the pattern edge. Use a heavy decorative thread in the upper looper and all-purpose or serger thread in the needle(s) and lower looper.

1. With the wrong side up, serge-finish the edge.

2. Fold the serged edge 7/8" to the wrong side.

3. Rethread the upper looper with serger thread. From the wrong side of the garment, serge along the fold without cutting it. If the width of your stitch is narrower than 1/4", straight-stitch 1/4" from the serged edge. (Fig. 5-9)

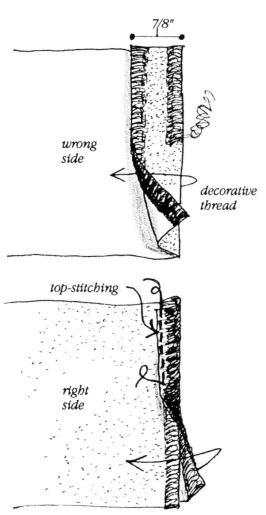

Fig. 5-9: *Fold the decorative edge to the wrong side and serge over the fold. Fold the edge back to the right side and top-stitch.*

4. Fold the decoratively serged edge to the right side (encasing the serged fold) and top-stitch to secure.

 Optional: Use fusible thread in the lower looper to add even more stability and eliminate the final top-stitching. Fuse to secure instead.

Project: Canvas Tote Bag

Serged self-binding stabilizes and decoratively finishes the top of this easy-to-make tote. A 42" length of 36"-wide or wider fabric makes two bags. (Fig. 5-10)

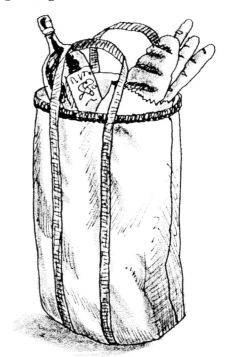

Fig. 5-10: *This canvas tote bag sports serged self-binding and webbing straps.*

Foot: Standard
Stitch: 3- or 3/4-thread
Stitch length: Short for decorative; standard N for serge-seaming
Stitch width: Widest
Thread: Contrasting color for decorative; matching for serge-seaming
Needle(s): All-purpose or serger
Upper looper: Cotton crochet thread for decorative; all-purpose or serger for serging fold and seaming
Lower looper: All-purpose or serger (fusible thread optional)
Tension: Balanced
Needle(s): Size 14/90
Fabric: 1-1/6 yards heavy cotton canvas or cotton duck
Notions: 3 yards of 1"-wide cotton webbing (if you want straps long enough to fit over your shoulder, you will need 3-3/4 yards)

1. Cut an 18" by 42" rectangle from the fabric.

2. Apply serged self-braid to the two short ends of the rectangle.

3. Fold the webbing into two equal lengths for the straps.

4. Fold 1-2" to the wrong side on each end of both straps. Place the straps on the right side of the bag piece 5-1/2" from each long side, as shown. (Fig. 5-11) Butt the folded edges together in the middle of the bag piece and top-stitch the webbing on both sides to secure. Reinforce the handles at the top edges of the bag by top-stitching square boxes, then cross-stitch diagonally. The handles will be

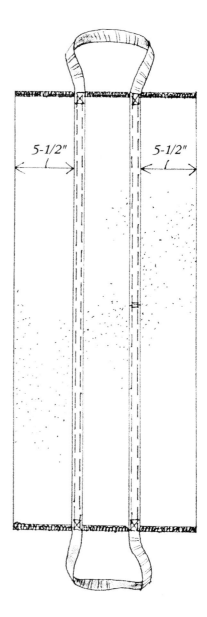

Fig. 5-11: *Position the straps on the bag. Top-stitch the edges. Reinforce with square boxes and cross-stitching.*

about 14", allowing the bag to be carried comfortably without dragging on the ground. If you purchase the longer webbing yardage to make a shoulder bag, the straps will be about 27".

5. With the right sides together, fold the bag piece in half, matching the short ends. Serge-seam both sides, matching the binding at the top edge. If you used a 3-thread stitch, reinforce the seams with straight-stitching.

6. From the inside of the bag, fold the corners to points with the serging in the middle, and straight-stitch a line 3" from the point, forming a triangle. (Fig. 5-12) This boxes the bottom of the bag.

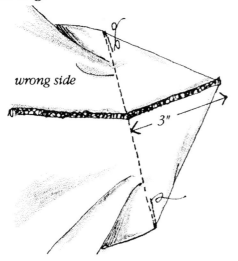

Fig. 5-12: *Straight-stitch the inside corners at the bottom of the bag.*

7. At the top edge, press the seam allowances to one side and top-stitch parallel to the decorative stitching to reinforce and secure.

Lesson 13. Double-bound Edge

In Lesson 2 (page 38), you learned how to serge a double-bound seam. Fabric is folded over the seam allowances and then decoratively serge-finished. A similar technique is used to create a double-bound edge. Consider using it to trim garment edges or home decoration projects.

A double-bound edge can be serged either directly onto the fabric or onto a binding strip for later application. This edge takes a little more time (just like double-bound seams), but it makes an attractive and durable trim.

1. Cut out the project leaving an extra 1" allowance for all edges that will be double-bound.

2. Fold or press 3/4" to the wrong side on each edge.

3. Adjust for a wide 3- or 3/4-thread stitch and a very short, satin-stitch length. A 7.5mm stitch width will produce a binding more than 1/2" wide (twice the stitch width).

4. With decorative thread in the upper looper and the turned-back fold of the fabric next to the knife, serge on the turned-back fold with the

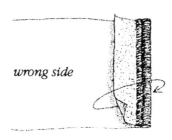

Fig. 5-13: Serge over the fold from the wrong side of the fabric to begin a double-bound edge. Fold the stitching to the right side and top-stitch.

wrong side of the fabric on top. (Fig. 5-13)

5. Press the serged fold to the right side of the fabric and top-stitch to secure.

 Optional: Use fusible thread in the lower looper, then fuse to secure.

6. Fold the cut edge of the fabric toward the wrong side, forming a fold the exact width as your previous stitching.

7. Serge over the fold with the needleline on top of or right next to the needleline of the previous stitching. (Fig. 5-14)

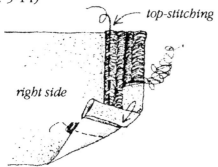

Fig. 5-14: Fold the cut edge toward the wrong side. Serge over the fold, matching needlines.

8. Trim away any excess allowance close to the stitching on the wrong side of the binding.

Project: Show-off Pillow

Double-bound edges accent a decorative inset piece on this fashionable pillow. We've embellished the contrasting inset fabric with diagonal rolled edges, but you may choose to show off any of your serger techniques. (Fig. 5-15)

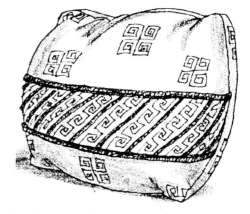

Fig. 5-15: A pillow with double-bound edges and a decorative inset shows off serging skills.

Foot: Standard for binding and serge-seaming; rolled edge for inset

Stitch: 3- or 3/4-thread for binding and serge-seaming; rolled edge for inset

Stitch length: Short

Stitch width: Widest for binding and seaming; narrow for rolled edge on inset

Thread: Contrasting color
Needles: All-purpose or serger
Upper looper: Woolly nylon
Lower looper: All-purpose or serger for binding and seaming; woolly nylon or monofilament nylon for rolled edge

Tension: Balanced for binding and serge-seaming; rolled edge for inset

Needle(s): Size 11/75

Fabric: 1/2 yard of velveteen or similar fabric; 1/4 yard of contrasting fabric for inset

Notions: 16" polyester pillow form

1. From the pillow fabric, cut one 16" by 16" square for the pillow back. Cut one 5" by 16" rectangle and one 8" by 16" rectangle for the pillow front. If you are using velveteen, make sure to cut all pieces with the nap going in the same direction.

2. Serge a double-bound edge along one long edge of both pillow front pieces. (Refer to the instructions on page 78.)

3. From the inset fabric, cut one 9" by 20" rectangle. Press-mark evenly spaced diagonal lines about 2-1/2" apart.

4. Adjust for a rolled-edge stitch and serge over all the press-marked lines.

5. Carefully press the decorated fabric. Cut the inset piece to a 6" by 16" rectangle.

6. Overlap each double-bound edge 1/2" over the long edges of the inset. Top-stitch to secure, completing the pillow front.

7. With the pillow front and the pillow back right sides together, serge-seam the edges with a wide, standard N-length, and balanced 3- or 3/4-thread stitch. Leave an 8" opening at the lower edge to insert the pillow form. Turn right side out. After inserting the pillow form, edge-stitch or hand-tack the opening closed.

Lesson 14. Serged Piping

Traditionally, piping is made by tightly covering a cord with fabric, leaving a seam allowance for inserting the piping into a garment or project seam. We can easily replicate traditional piping by serging over filler cord onto a strip of 1-1/4"-wide bias tricot, such as *Seams Great*.

1. Thread the upper looper with decorative thread and adjust for a rolled edge with a short, satin-length stitch.

2. Serge over one or more strands of heavy thread or cording. Place the filler under the back and over the front of the foot, or use the beading or ribbon foot to help guide it. Refer back to Lesson 4 (page 50) for tips on serging over filler cord.

 Special Tips: If your rolled edge is not completely wrapping to the underside, use monofilament or woolly nylon thread in the lower looper. You may need to increase the stitch width if you are serging over several strands of heavy thread or a thick cord. You might also need to increase the stitch length if you have heavy decorative thread in your upper looper.

3. Serge over the filler for several inches, then insert the bias tricot strip under the presser foot. Serge over the strip, trimming about 1/2" with the knives. Do not stretch while serging. At the end, raise the presser foot, clear the stitch finger, and chain off over the filler.

4. Insert the piping into a garment or project seam using a straight-stitch and a zipper foot.

The filler cord itself may also be used as an ornamental element. Serge over decorative thread, ribbon, or braid using monofilament nylon in the upper looper and a longer stitch length. (Fig. 5-16)

Elasticized piping

Create a stretchable serged piping for stretch and knit garments by using clear elastic in place of the bias tricot. Stretch the elastic slightly while serge-piping along one edge.

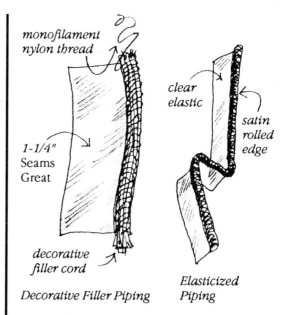

Decorative Filler Piping   *Elasticized Piping*

Fig. 5-16: *Serged piping options include featuring the filler cord itself and stretchable piping.*

For maximum coverage, use woolly nylon in the upper looper. (Fig. 5-17)

For more pronounced elasticized piping, serge over a strand of elastic cording as well as the transparent

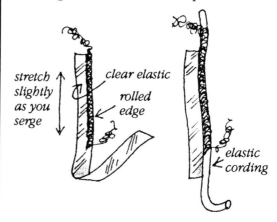

Fig. 5-17: *Serge onto clear elastic to make elasticized piping. Add elastic cording under the stitches for a more pronounced effect.*

elastic. Thread the elastic cording over the front and under the back of the presser foot (or use a beading or ribbon foot) when serging over the transparent elastic. Be careful not to cut the cording. After making the piping, pull the elastic cording until it lays smoothly.

 Special Tip: When serging over elastic cording, test first—you may need to tighten the upper looper tension so that the thread tightly covers the cording.

Mock piping

Like serged piping, mock piping is made by covering an edge or seamline (with or without filler cord) with a satin rolled edge. It is not considered actual piping, however, because it is serged directly onto the fabric instead of being applied to a bias strip and inserted into a seam. We often see mock piping used as a decorative detail on lightweight robes, pajamas, and casual wear.

To create a simple mock-piped edge, serge along the right side of the fabric using a satin rolled edge. Mock piping can be serged single-layer on more stable fabrics or double-layer (wrong sides together). (Fig. 5-18)

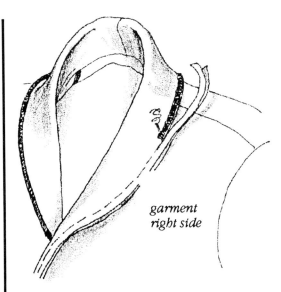

garment right side

Fig. 5-18: *Create mock piping by serge-finishing the edges, wrong sides together, with a satin rolled edge.*

On lightweight material, the fabric edge will roll inside the stitching, creating a piped appearance without filler cord. On heavier fabrics, it may not be possible to roll the edge. In this case, loosen the upper looper and adjust for a narrow, satin-length, reversible-edge binding stitch (page 66). Inserting filler cord will add to the piped effect.

A variation of the mock-piped edge is used to create mock-piped bands and cuffs on lightweight fabrics.

1. Fold the band or cuff lengthwise with wrong sides together.

2. Place the band to the wrong side of the fabric, matching the cut edges.

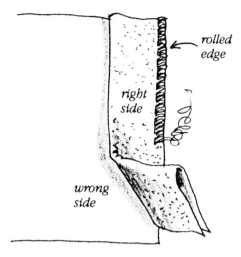

Fig. 5-19: *For mock piping, place the wrong side of the band against the wrong side of the fabric. Serge-seam with a satin rolled edge.*

3. Serge mock piping with the band on top. (Fig. 5-19)

4. Pull the seam flat and press the allowances away from the band or cuff.

Another mock-piping variation can be used to hem sleeves and lower edges.

1. Lightly press 1/4" to the wrong side. Then press the hem allowance to the wrong side. This technique looks best with a hem allowance of 1" or more. If the hem allowance on your pattern is narrower, add a wider allowance when cutting out the project.

2. Make another fold to the wrong side equal to the hem allowance, sandwiching the 1/4" edge toward the inside of the fold, as shown. (Fig. 5-20)

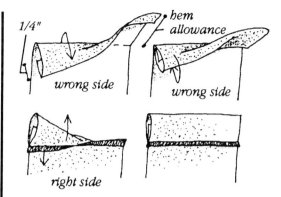

Fig. 5-20: *For a mock-piped hem, press 1/4" and then the hem allowance to the wrong side. Fold again and serge with a satin rolled edge. Pull the seam flat.*

3. From the right side, serge over the fold with the satin rolled edge, being careful not to cut the fabric.

4. Pull the seam flat and press the allowances away from the folded hem edge. The cut edge will be encased inside the hem.

Elasticized mock piping

Mock piping provides a stable, decorative edge-finish for a neckline or armscye. If the edge needs to stretch with movement, however, such as on swimsuits and exercise-wear, you'll need elasticized mock piping. (Fig. 5-17, page 81)

To apply elasticized mock piping to a neckline:

1. Trim away the neckline seam allowance. Serge-seam one shoulder.

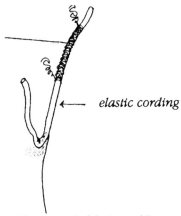

Fig. 5-21: *Finish a stretch-fabric neckline or armscye by serging elasticized piping directly onto the fabric.*

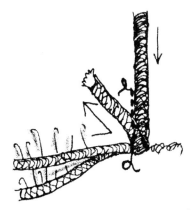

Fig. 5-22: *Serge the remaining seam, folding the cording back. Straight-stitch over the needleline to secure before trimming the tail.*

2. Insert elastic cording under the back and over the front of the presser foot (or use a beading or ribbon foot), and serge a few stitches over the cording. Then place the fabric right side up under the cording and serge the neckline edge. Stretch the cording slightly as you serge.

3. Serge-seam the other shoulder, folding the elastic cording back toward the garment and serging over it as you complete the seam. (Fig. 5-22) Be careful not to cut the cording. Straight-stitch over the cording to secure it before trimming the end.

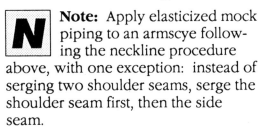

Note: Apply elasticized mock piping to an armscye following the neckline procedure above, with one exception: instead of serging two shoulder seams, serge the shoulder seam first, then the side seam.

Project: Serge-piped Book Cover

Cover your current paperback book with style. Serged piping accents the upper and lower edges. A matching satin rolled edge finishes the inner edges. (Fig. 5-23)

Fig. 5-23: *Make an easy paperback book cover featuring contrasting piping. Give one as a thoughtful gift or show it off yourself.*

Foot: Beading, ribbon, or standard for piping and trim; standard for serge-finishing

Stitch: 3-thread for rolled-edge piping and trim; 3- or 3/4-thread for serge-finishing

Stitch length: Short for piping and trim; standard N for serge-finishing

Stitch width: Narrow for piping and trim; standard N or wider for serge-finishing

Thread: Contrasting color
Needle(s): All-purpose or serger
Upper looper: #8 pearl cotton for piping and trim; all-purpose or serger for serge-finishing
Lower looper: Monofilament nylon for piping and trim; all-purpose or serger for serge-finishing

Filler: 4 strands of #5 pearl cotton, the same color as the upper looper thread

Tension: Rolled edge for piping and trim; balanced for serge-finishing

Needle(s): Size 14/90

Fabric: 1/4 yard denim

Notions: 2 yards of 1-1/4" *Seams Great*; 10" of 3/8"-wide ribbon to match the piping (for a book mark)

1. Cut a 16-1/2" by 8" rectangle from the denim.

2. With matching thread and a wide balanced stitch, serge-finish both long edges.

3. With a satin-length, rolled-edge stitch and decorative thread in the upper looper, serge-finish both short

ends of the rectangle, creating a trim.

4. Using the same stitch, serge over the four strands of #5 pearl cotton onto the *Seams Great* to make at least 24" of serged piping.

5. For the upper edge, center an 11" section of piping along the 1/4" seamline on the right side of one long edge. (Fig. 5-24)

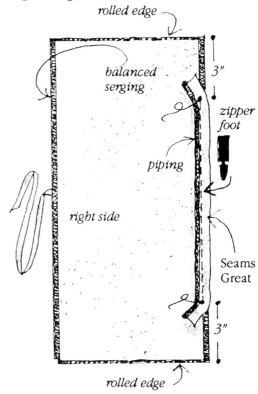

rolled edge

balanced serging

3"

zipper foot

piping

right side

Seams Great

3"

rolled edge

Fig. 5-24: *Straight-stitch the piping along the 1/4" seamline, starting and ending 3" from each end.*

6. Matching cut edges, pin one end of the ribbon on the wrong side at the center of the edge.

7. Using a zipper foot, straight-stitch next to the piping, starting and ending 3" from each end. You will have about 1" tails of serged piping extending past the stitching.

8. Repeat steps 5 and 7 for the lower edge. (Skip step 6.)

9. Fold 3" to the right side on each end. Matching the cut edges, straight-stitch over the piping stitching line, pulling the piping tails in the direction of the seam allowances at each corner. (Fig. 5-25)

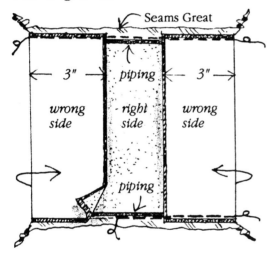

Fig. 5-25: *Fold back the cover pockets and straight-stitch over the piping stitching line. Pull the piping tails to the wrong side of the seamline.*

10. Trim the *Seams Great* close to the stitching. Turn the cover to the right side and top-stitch next to the piping along the upper and lower edges.

Lesson 15.
Serged Binding

It is often difficult to find just the right decorative trim for your fashion or project. Now you have a wide range of options for designing and serging your own. The base fabric width, content, and color can be varied. And you can use a large assortment of thread types and colors. Any decorative edging stitch is a possibility. Always test first.

1. Select a bias strip of woven fabric or a cross-grain strip of knit that matches or contrasts with the fabric you are binding. Cut the length you'll need plus 1". The width of the bias strip should measure your desired finished trim width plus 1/2". For a 3/4"-wide trim, you'll need a strip 1-1/4" wide.

2. On one long edge, press 1/4" to the wrong side.

3. Adjust your serger for a balanced 3-thread stitch or any other decorative stitch you would like on your trim.

4. With decorative thread in the upper looper and the fold next to the knife, serge carefully along the fold without cutting the fabric. Use the blindhem foot for accurate guiding.

 Special Tip: For the easiest finishing, use fusible thread in the lower looper and a medium to wide, balanced stitch.

5. Place the decorative side of the strip against the wrong side of the project fabric, aligning the cut edges.

6. Using all-purpose or serger thread, serge the edge with a 1/4" seam. If your stitch is not that wide, serge-seam first, then straight-stitch at the 1/4" seamline. (Fig. 5-26)

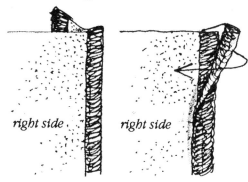

right side   *right side*

Fig. 5-26: Decoratively serge the binding strip, using fusible thread in the lower looper. Serge-seam the strip to the fabric, then wrap decorative serging to the right side and fuse.

7. Wrap the trim to the right side, encasing the seam.

8. Carefully press the trim in place and top-stitch to secure. If you've used fusible thread, carefully fuse the trim in place. Then top-stitching is optional, but it will add durability.

9. To add more texture or color to your trim, you may choose to use a wider binding and decoratively serge over the folded edge (without cutting it). Use a different stitch or stitch width for variety. (Fig. 5-27)

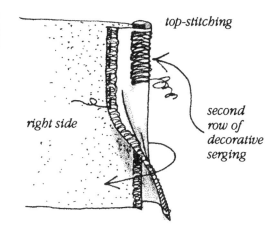

top-stitching

right side

second row of decorative serging

Fig. 5-27: Add more color and texture to serged binding with a wider strip. Then decoratively serge again after folding and securing the binding on the right side.

Project: Serge-bound Table Runner

Add elegance to a special dinner party with an easily constructed table runner. It is neatly finished with a narrow, serged binding trim. A tassel ornaments each end. (Fig. 5-28)

Fig. 5-28: Metallic serged binding highlights an easy, yet elegant, table runner.

Foot: Standard
Stitch: 3-thread for decorative; 3- or 3/4-thread for serge-seaming
Stitch length: Short for decorative; standard N for serge-seaming
Stitch width: Widest
Thread: Contrasting color
    Needle(s): All-purpose or serger
    Upper looper: Metallic yarn for decorative; all-purpose or serger for serge-seaming
    Lower looper: All-purpose, serger, or fusible for decorative; all-purpose or serger for serge-seaming
Tension: Balanced
Needle(s): Size 14/75
Fabric: 2 yards tapestry or heavy brocade for 70" length (or 2-1/2 yards for a 90" length); one yard matching lightweight satin for binding

1. Cut a 20" by 70" or 90" rectangle (depending on the measurements of your table) from the runner fabric.

2. Fold the fabric in half lengthwise. At each end, fold the corner back and press-mark a bias line. (Fig. 5-29) Cut on this line to form the end points.

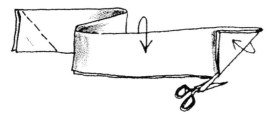

Fig. 5-29: *Fold the fabric lengthwise, then align the short edges back against the folds and press-mark. Cut on the press marks to form points.*

3. Cut and splice 1-1/4"-wide bias strips of the matching lightweight satin to make a trim the length of the runner perimeter plus 1". On one long edge, carefully press 1/4" to the wrong side.

4. Adjust your serger for a short, wide, balanced stitch and decoratively serge the folded edge.

5. Along one side of the table runner (from point to point), serge the cut edge of the right side of the trim to the wrong side of the fabric. If your serger does not have a 1/4" seaming width, straight-stitch on the 1/4" seamline after serge-seaming. Wrap the binding to the right side and top-stitch. (Fig. 5-30)

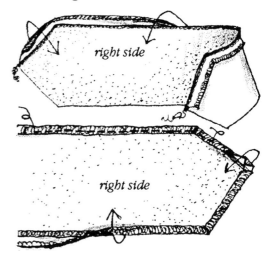

Fig. 5-30: *Apply serged binding to one side of the runner. Serge-seam the opposite edge. Fold back the corners to miter before top-stitching.*

Optional: Use fusible thread in the lower looper of the decorative stitching and fuse instead of top-stitching.

6. Repeat step 5 for the opposite edge of the runner. Before wrapping the binding to the right side, fold back the corners on each end to form miters. Then top-stitch to secure.

7. Cover the end points and reinforce them with tassels by following the instructions in Lesson 35 (page 155).

Lesson 16.
Serge-piped Binding

A popular variation of the serged piping in Lesson 14 is constructed with a narrow rolled edge and a satin-stitch length. This binding gives the appearance of piping without the extra steps of inserting a piping strip. Serge-piped binding makes a pretty, delicate finish on lightweight or silky fabric—great for neckline and sleeve edges.

1. Cut a bias strip of woven fabric or a cross-grain strip of knit for the binding. Cut the length you'll need plus 1". The width of the bias strip should measure your desired finished

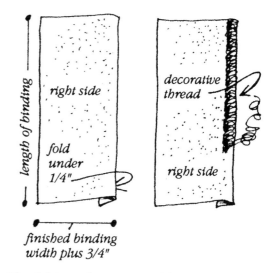

Fig. 5-31: Make serge-piped binding by pressing 1/4" to the wrong side and serging a rolled edge on the fold.

trim width plus 3/4". For a 1/2" finished binding, cut the binding strips 1-1/4" wide.

2. On one long edge, press 1/4" to the wrong side. (Fig. 5-31)

3. Serge-finish the fold with a narrow rolled edge adjusted to a short, satin-stitch length. Use decorative thread in the upper looper and matching all-purpose or serger thread in the needle and lower looper. Shiny rayon thread is a good choice for silky fabric because it complements the fabric texture.

4. Place the right side of the binding to the wrong side of the project fabric with cut edges matching.

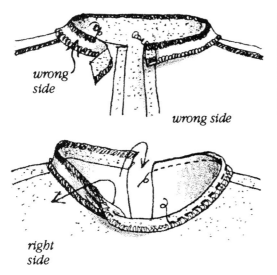

wrong side

wrong side

right side

Fig. 5-32: *Serge the binding to the wrong side of the edge. Wrap it to the right side and straight-stitch along the rolled-edge needleline.*

5. Serge a 1/4" seam. (Fig. 5-32) If your widest serged stitch is narrower than 1/4", straight-stitch at the 1/4" seamline after serge-seaming.

6. Fold the binding to the right side and straight-stitch on top of the rolled-edge needleline. Use a zipper foot to help position your stitches accurately.

Project: Padded Picture Frame

Serge-piped binding finishes the inside oval edge of this pretty 5" by 7" picture frame. Enlarge the measurements to fit a larger photo. (The binding is more difficult to apply for a frame smaller than 5" by 7".) (Fig. 5-33)

Fig. 5-33: *A padded picture frame is trimmed with serge-piped binding.*

Foot: Rolled edge for decorative; standard for serge-finishing
Stitch: Rolled edge for decorative; 3-thread for serge-finishing
Stitch length: Satin for decorative; short for serge-finishing
Stitch width: Narrow
Thread: Contrasting color
    Needle: All-purpose or serger
    Upper looper: Rayon for decorative; all-purpose or serger for serge-finishing
    Lower looper: Woolly nylon for decorative; all-purpose or serger for serge-finishing
Tension: Rolled edge for decorative; balanced for serge-finishing
Needle: Size 11/75
Fabric: 1/3 yard 45"-wide woven
Notions: 1/4 yard fusible transfer web; 8" by 10" polyester bonded

batting; one file folder; 6" by 8" of 1/8"-thick cardboard; 5-3/4" by 7-3/4" clear acetate sheet (from a school- or office-supply store); glue gun and glue

1. From the fabric, cut two 8" by 10" rectangles, one 6" by 8" rectangle, and one bias strip 1-1/4" by 18". From the transfer web, cut one 8" by 10" rectangle and one 5-1/2" by 7-1/2" rectangle.

2. To make the frame, cut a 6" by 8" rectangle from the file folder. Cut a 4" by 6" oval opening in the center of the rectangle, as shown. (Fig. 5-34)

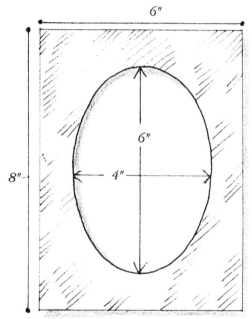

Fig. 5-34: From the file folder, cut a rectangle with an oval in the center.

3. Center and fuse together one 8" by 10" fabric piece, the 8" by 10" transfer web, the batting, the 5-1/2" by 7-1/2" transfer web, and the cardboard frame, as shown. (Fig. 5-35)

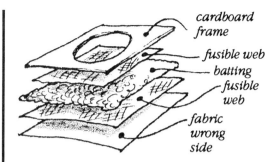

Fig. 5-35: Fuse the layers to the front of the frame. Cut out along the oval edge after fusing.

4. Cut out the batting and fabric inside the oval, right at the opening edge. Fold the fused layers to the back of the frame on all four outer edges and glue in place.

5. For the binding, press 1/4" to the wrong side along one long edge of the bias strip. With decorative thread in the upper looper, serge-finish over the fold with a rolled-edge stitch. Serge about 6" of extra chain, leaving thread tails at the ends. The chain will be used for hanging the finished picture frame.

6. On one short end, fold the bias strip 3/8" to the wrong side. On the file-folder side, beginning at the lower right edge of the oval, place the right side of the folded end of the binding against the frame, matching the cut edges. Straight-stitch the binding to the frame around the oval opening using a 1/4" seam allowance. (You will be stitching through the file folder, as well as through the fabric and batting.) Lap the end of the strip over the beginning fold as you complete the seam. (Fig. 5-36)

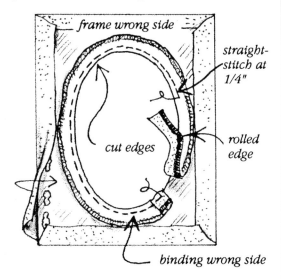

Fig. 5-36: *Sew the right side of the binding to the wrong side of the frame.*

7. Fold the binding evenly to the right side. Straight-stitch on the rolled-edge needleline to secure.

8. Make the frame back by folding the other 8" by 10" fabric piece over the heavier cardboard. Glue the edges on the wrong side to secure.

9. With a narrow, balanced 3-thread stitch, serge-finish the 6" by 8" fabric piece, trimming approximately 1/8" from all sides. Glue the serge-finished piece over the fabric edges on the cardboard back.

10. Use the rolled-edge chain made in step 5 for hanging. Hand-tack each end to the serge-finishing stitches on both sides of the frame back, about 2-1/2" down from the top edge.

11. Apply glue around two sides and the bottom of both frame pieces—on the front side of the covered cardboard and the back side of the frame front. Keep the glue within 1/4" of the edge. Sandwich the clear acetate between the two glued pieces and apply pressure until dry. (Fig. 5-37)

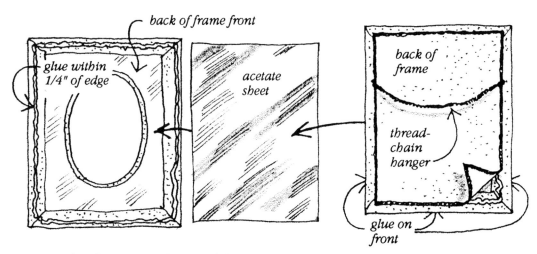

Fig. 5-37: *Glue the sides and bottom of the frame pieces, sandwiching the acetate sheet between.*

12. Cover the binding overlap with the flower made in Lesson 24 (page 116) and complete the frame.

Lesson 17.
Double Rolled-edge Braid and Binding

The double rolled edge featured in Lesson 5 (page 54) can be adapted to make both a narrow braid and a decorative binding. Using contrasting thread colors for the two rolled edges accents the delicate technique. Because maximum thread coverage and a perfectly rolled edge are important, we often choose woolly nylon for both the upper and lower loopers.

Double rolled-edge braid

To make double rolled-edge braid for trimming your garments, home decorations, or craft projects, serge over a 1/2" strip of base fabric. Choose any lightweight fabric that matches or blends with the upper looper thread color.

1. Adjust your serger for a satin rolled edge.

2. Serge one long edge of the fabric strip, leaving a thread chain several inches long.

3. Rethread the upper looper with a contrasting-color thread. Serge the other side of the strip with the needle on, or right next to, the needleline of

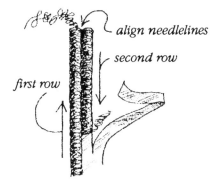

Fig. 5-38: *Make a double rolled-edge braid trim by serging two rows of rolled edging on a fabric strip, aligning the needlelines.*

the original serging. (Fig. 5-38) Hold the thread chain taut to start the serging without jamming. Aligning the needlelines and perfecting this technique may take a little practice.

4. Top-stitch the braid to your project fabric, stitching directly on the center needleline.

Double rolled-edge binding

Make a matching decorative binding by serge-finishing the folded edge of a bias-woven or a cross-grain knit binding strip using a double rolled-edge technique. Choose a lightweight fabric that matches or blends with the thread colors and the fabric to be bound.

1. Cut and splice the binding strip twice your finished binding width plus 1-1/2" by the length you'll need for your project. Fold the strip in half lengthwise with wrong sides together.

2. Serge the fold with a satin rolled edge. From the wrong side, press the binding open.

3. Rethread the upper looper with a contrasting-color thread. Then refold the binding strip and serge-finish the edge with the needlelines on top of, or right next to, each other. (Fig. 5-39)

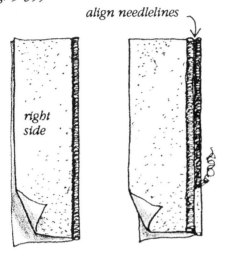

align needlelines

right side

Fig. 5-39: *For double rolled-edge binding, serge-finish a fold. Then refold and serge an adjoining rolled edge.*

Optional: For a wider trim, cut the strip wider and serge three or more rows. Allow about 3/8" of fabric for each additional rolled-edge row.

4. Place the right side of the binding to the wrong side of the fabric, matching the cut edges. Serge-seam with your widest stitch or straight-stitch a 1/4" seam. If you are applying the binding to an outside curve, ease the binding around the curve.

5. Press the binding to the right side and top-stitch between the rolled-edge rows to secure. (Fig. 5-40)

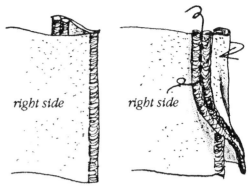

right side   *right side*

Fig. 5-40: *Serge-seam double rolled-edge binding to the fabric edge. Wrap it to the right side and top-stitch on the center needleline.*

Project:
Tooth Fairy Pillow

Double rolled-edge binding finishes the pocket and edges of this special little pillow. The tooth fairy will know just where to find the lost tooth and leave a reward. (Fig. 5-41)

Fig. 5-41: *This special tooth fairy pillow is trimmed with double rolled-edge binding.*

Foot: Rolled edge for decorative; standard for serge-seaming

Stitch: Rolled edge for decorative; 3- or 3/4-thread for serge-seaming

Stitch length: Short for decorative; standard N for serge-seaming

Stitch width: Narrow for decorative; widest for serge-seaming

Thread: Contrasting colors
   Needle(s): All-purpose or serger
   Upper looper: Two contrasting colors of woolly nylon for decorative; all-purpose or serger for serge-seaming
   Lower looper: Woolly nylon for decorative; all-purpose or serger for serge-seaming

Tension: Rolled edge for decorative; balanced for serge-seaming

Needle(s): Size 11/75

Fabric: 1/6 yard 45"-wide woven; 2-1/2" by 27" matching or contrasting bias strip

Notions: Approximately one handful of polyester fiberfill; 12" of 1/8"-wide ribbon for bow

1. Cut two 4-1/2" by 5-1/2" rectangles for the pillow and one 4-1/2" by 3-1/2" rectangle for the pocket. Place the pocket over the two pillow pieces and match the cut edges at one end. Using a cup, round all four corners. (Fig. 5-42)

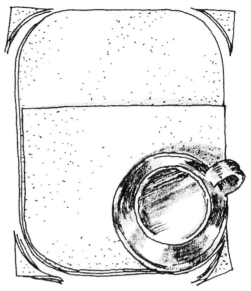

Fig. 5-42: *Place the smaller rectangle over the two larger rectangles and round the corners.*

2. Make double rolled-edge binding on the bias strip following the instructions on pages 93 - 94. Trim the strip width to 1".

3. Bind the upper (straight) edge of the pocket by applying the right side of the binding to the wrong side of the pocket. Wrap the binding to the right side and top-stitch on the rolled-edge needleline.

4. Place the pillow pieces wrong sides together with the pocket on top, matching the cut edges. Serge-seam around the pillow with a wide, balanced stitch. Leave an opening at the top for inserting the fiberfill. Stuff the pillow and serge-seam the opening closed.

5. On one short end, fold the binding strip 1/2" to the wrong side. Beginning in the middle of the top edge, place the right side of the folded end of the binding against the back side of the pillow, matching the cut edges. Serge with a 1/4" seam allowance, lapping the end of the strip over the beginning fold as you complete the seam. If your serger does not have a stitch that wide, straight-stitch on the 1/4" seamline after serging.

6. Fold the binding to the right side and top-stitch on the rolled-edge needleline to secure.

7. Add a bow at the top of the pillow to cover the binding joint.

Lesson 18. Elasticized Trims and Binding

The serger makes sewing stretch and knit fabrics a breeze. Now you can also serge elasticized trims and binding to add decorative detail and to individualize your garments.

Elasticized trims

A classic example of new products leading to new techniques, serging elasticized trim was never an option before the introduction of clear elastic. Now we can make a variety of stretch trims to coordinate with any stretch or knit fabric. Using different stitch widths, tension adjustments, and thread types adds to the possibilities.

Because clear elastic is so lightweight, it is important to serge through it to keep it from rolling. Neatly trim any excess elastic after serging the trim. The *Hobbylock* elastic foot works best for 3/8"- and 1/2"-width elastic. Loosen the foot's screw so that no tension is placed on the elastic.

Single-stretch Trim

1. Begin with a single row of serging on a piece of clear elastic. Test various widths.

2. Adjust the stitch width to the width of braid desired. The elastic width must be wider than the stitch width.

3. Serge, using a short (not satin), 2mm stitch length. For better coverage, use woolly nylon in both loopers.

4. Adjust the tension for a balanced 3-thread stitch, making it loose enough to allow the elastic to lie flat. After serging several inches, test the braid by stretching. If the stitches break, loosen the needle thread tension or stretch the elastic slightly as you serge.

5. If you're not using an elastic foot, hold the elastic taut in front of and behind the presser foot while serging. It is not necessary to stretch the elastic because the serged stitch allows for stretch.

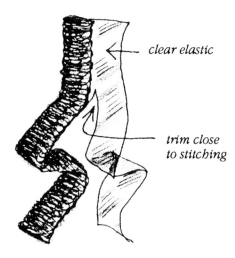

clear elastic

trim close
to stitching

Fig. 5-43: *Decoratively serge clear elastic, then trim it close to the stitching to make single stretch trim.*

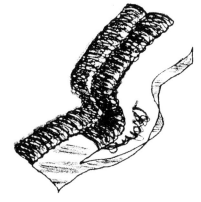

Fig. 5-44: *Double-stretch trim features a second row of serging with needlelines aligned.*

6. Trim the elastic close to the serging, being careful not to cut the stitches. (Fig. 5-43) If part of the elastic still remains, it won't show after the trim is top-stitched to the garment.

7. Top-stitch the trim to the garment using a long straight-stitch or a very narrow zigzag and sewing close to each edge of the trim. Stretch the elastic as you sew.

Double-stretch Trim

Select an elastic that is wider than the trim you will be making.

1. Serge one side of the elastic following the above guidelines, but do not trim the elastic.

2. On the opposite (unserged) side, serge another row with the needle just inside or next to the needleline of the previous stitching. (Fig. 5-44) For variation, use a different thread color in the upper looper when serging the second side.

3. Top-stitch the trim to the garment using a long stitch and sewing close to each edge of the trim. Stretch the elastic as you sew.

Stretch-trim Variations

Adjust your serger for a narrow, balanced stitch. Tighten the lower looper tension slightly. Serge the elastic, following the directions for the double-stretch trim.

Try serging a balanced stitch on one side and a rolled-edge stitch on the other side. Or serge a rolled edge on both sides, overlapping the needle-lines. (Fig. 5-45) For more elasticity when serging a rolled edge on clear elastic, stretch the elastic. It will return to its original length after serging.

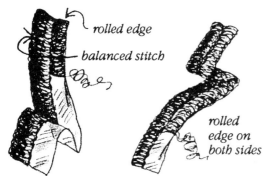

rolled edge

balanced stitch

rolled edge on both sides

Fig. 5-45: *Stretch-trim variations include double trim with one or two rolled edges.*

Braided Trim

Braid the elastic trim for swimsuit or camisole straps:

1. Serge a strand of single-stretch trim six times the length of the strap plus 6".

2. Cut the trim into six equal lengths. Braid it into two straps and secure the ends with straight-stitching. (Fig. 5-46)

3. Attach the straps to your garment according to the pattern guidesheet.

Elasticized binding

This technique adds stretch and stability to an edge and creates a neat, decorative binding at the same time.

Fig. 5-46: *Braided stretch trim is used for swimsuit and camisole straps.*

You have the option of leaving one serged-finished edge exposed on the under side of the binding or wrapping and twin-needle top-stitching to leave no serged edges exposed.

Elasticized binding works especially well on stretch fabrics because the serged stitch used to apply the elastic is a stretch stitch. Use it to finish the edges of swim or exercisewear. You can even extend the binding past the garment edge to form straps.

Any width elastic can be used, but 3/8" is the most versatile. Select any type except clear elastic. (It will roll inside the binding.)

To bind the edge of stretch fabric:

1. Cut the elastic to the desired length. Cut a stretch binding strip the same length. Its width should be three times the width of the elastic plus 1/4". For a heavy or thick fabric, cut the strip an additional 1/4" wider.

2. Serge-finish one long edge of the strip using a standard-N width and length 3-thread stitch, trimming only slightly to neaten.

3. Place the right sides of the binding and fabric together, matching the cut edges. Straight-stitch with a seam allowance the width of the elastic (usually 3/8"). Stretch the layers as you sew. (Fig. 5-47)

4. Adjust the serger for a long, balanced 3-thread stitch. Place the elastic on top of the binding, next to the

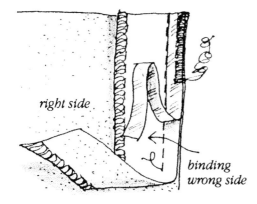

Fig. 5-47: For elasticized binding, straight-stitch the binding to the garment, stretching both layers. Serge elastic to the seam allowance on top of the binding.

edge. Serge it to the seam allowance through all layers.

5. Fold the binding to the wrong side, encasing the serged seam allowance. From the right side, top-stitch on the binding with a narrow zigzag or a twin needle to secure, stretching slightly as you sew. (Fig. 5-48) Or stitch-in-the-ditch from the right side, stretching firmly.

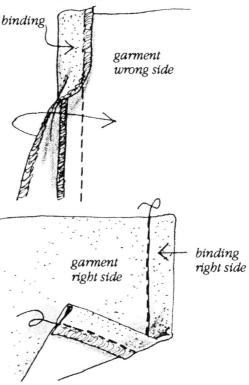

Fig. 5-48: Fold the binding to the wrong side and top-stitch or stitch-in-the-ditch.

 Optional: To make a binding with no exposed serging, the width of the binding strip should be four times the width of the elastic plus 1/4". Don't serge-finish one long edge. After applying (steps 3 and 4), fold the unsewn edge of the binding 3/8" (the width of the seam allowance) to the wrong side, matching the cut edge to the serged edge. Fold 3/8" again, encasing the serged elastic. From the right side, top-stitch as in step 5. (Fig. 5-49)

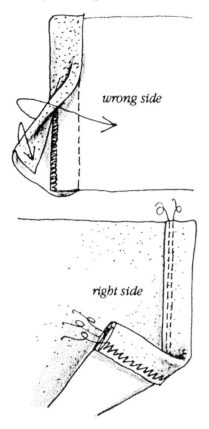

Fig. 5-49: *For elasticized binding with no exposed serging, fold the unsewn edge to the wrong side and wrap it to encase the elastic. Top-stitch or stitch-in-the-ditch to secure.*

The application of elasticized binding varies slightly from stretch fabrics to wovens. When elasticized binding is applied to the edge of woven fabric, the fabric is gathered in with the

elastic, so the fabric and binding must be cut larger than the opening.

1. Cut the elastic smaller than the opening, to the desired length.

2. If you are applying the binding to a curved area, cut the trim strip on the bias to allow it to lie smoothly.

3. Straight-stitch the binding to the fabric without stretching.

4. When applying the elastic, stretch the elastic to fit the length of the binding as you serge.

5. Finish as instructed for the stretch binding.

Project: Ruffled Jar Cover

Serged elastic trim tucks this decorative cover around any jar lid. A ribbon bow adds a pretty finishing touch. (Fig. 5-50)

Fig. 5-50: *This ruffled jar cover has serged clear-elastic trim.*

Foot: Elastic or standard for elastic trim; rolled edge for serge-finishing

Stitch: 3-thread

Stitch length: Short

Stitch width: Narrow

Thread: Contrasting color
  Needle: All-purpose or serger
  Upper looper: Woolly nylon
  Lower looper: All-purpose or serger

Tension: Balanced for braid trim; rolled edge for serge-finishing

Needle: Size 11/75

Fabric: 1/4 yard gingham (or 8" by 8" square)

Notions: 12" of 1/4"- or 3/8"-wide clear elastic; 12" of 1/8"-wide ribbon; air-erasable marker

1. Cut an 8" circle from the gingham, using a lid or plate as a guide. With a smaller lid, mark a 5-1/2" circle inside the larger one using an air-erasable marker.

2. Serge-finish the edge of the larger circle with a rolled edge.

3. Serge along one edge of the elastic with a narrow satin stitch. If available, use an elastic foot with the tension screw loosened. Trim the unsewn elastic close to the serging.

4. Pin-mark the inner circle in halves and the elastic trim at 3-1/2" and 7". Place the elastic on the circle and straight-stitch through it with a long stitch, stretching to fit the markings. (Fig. 5-51) Finish by lapping the end over the beginning of the trim.

5. Tie the ribbon into a bow and hand-tack it over the joined ends of the elastic.

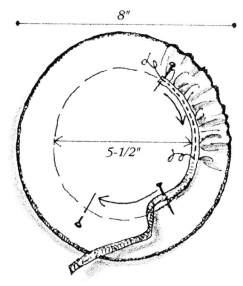

Fig. 5-51: Stretch the clear elastic trim while top-stitching.

Lesson 19. Tear-away Braid

Make a simple, balanced braid by serging over tear-away stabilizer using decorative thread (such as pearl cotton) and a satin-stitch length. Serge-decorate one or both edges of the braid or join several widths together using a narrow zigzag.

1. Adjust for a wide, satin-length, and balanced 3-thread stitch using pearl cotton or another heavy decorative thread in the loopers and all-purpose or serger thread in the needle. (To prevent jamming, remember to begin with a standard N stitch length and shorten it as needed to perfect the satin stitch.)

2. Serge over a strip of tear-away stabilizer the length of braid you'll need. (Fig. 5-52) You may need to lap the short ends of several strips of the stabilizer.

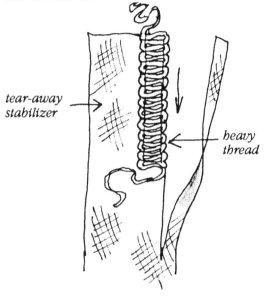

tear-away stabilizer →

← *heavy thread*

Fig. 5-52: *Serge a chunky braid over tear-away stabilizer.*

Fig. 5-53: *Zigzag together two or more rows of tear-away braid. Edge with serged-on picot braid if desired.*

3. Straight-stitch over both long edges and tear away the stabilizer.

Make a braid of any width by placing two or more braid strands side by side and joining them with a zigzag stitch. Use matching or monofilament nylon thread in the needle of a narrow zigzag for nearly invisible seaming, or use a contrasting color and a wider zigzag for a decorative effect. (Fig. 5-53) For a decorative edge on either single- or multiple-width tear-away braid, serge one or both edges from the wrong side with a picot-braid edge (see page 52).

 Optional: For fusible tear-away braid, use fusible thread in the lower looper, adjusting so that the decorative thread just wraps the edge and the fusible thread is not visible from the right side of the braid. Or, use fusible thread in the bobbin when straight-stitching the braid edges and, for multiple strands, also use fusible thread in the bobbin of the zigzag stitch. Fuse the braid to the fabric, using a press cloth. If desired, top-stitch for added durability.

Project: Pretty Pencil Cup

Decorate your desk or telephone area with a color-coordinated pencil cup. Your serged tear-away braid is displayed for all to see. (Fig. 5-54)

Fig. 5-54: Store pens and pencils in a handy pencil cup decorated with tear-away braid.

Foot: Standard
Stitch: 3-thread for braid; 3- or 3/4-thread for serge-finishing
Stitch length: Satin for braid; standard N for serge-finishing
Stitch width: Widest for braid; standard N for serge-finishing
Thread: Contrasting for braid; matching for serge-finishing
Needle: All-purpose or serger
Upper looper: 3 colors of heavy decorative for braid; all-purpose or serger for serge-finishing
Lower looper: 3 colors of heavy decorative for braid; all-purpose or serger for serge-finishing
Tension: Balanced
Needle: Size 14/90
Fabric: 1/6 yard
Notions: One 4" by 30" strip tear-away stabilizer (lap several pieces if necessary); one metal can; all-purpose craft glue

1. Cut a fabric rectangle the circumference of the can plus 1" by the height of the can. Serge-finish all edges.

2. Wrap and glue the fabric around the can, turning under the serging on the overlapping layer. (Fig. 5-55)

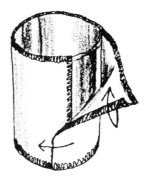

Fig. 5-55: Glue the fabric to the cup, turning under the serging on one vertical edge before overlapping the other.

3. Serge three different-colored rows of tear-away braid, following the previous instructions. The rows should be *at least* twice the circumference of the can plus 2".

4. Zigzag the three rows together to form one long strand of braid.

5. Cut two strands of braid the exact circumference of the can and glue them in place on the upper and lower edges.

Lesson 20.
Puffed Serged Braid

A thread chain serged from heavy decorative thread can be used as ornamental braid. Serging over several strands of filler (as described in previous lessons) makes a heavier braid. For an even chunkier, puffed braid, serge over rolled fabric or thick yarn.

A strip of 1"-wide tricot, T-shirt knit, or jersey (cut on the crosswise grain) can be used for the puff-braid filler. Or use 5/8"-wide *Seams Great* for a more delicate braid. When pulled, the fabric strip rolls into a narrow tube and serger stitches can be formed around it. The resulting puffed braid is ideal for edging, couching, and craft projects.

Use decorative thread in the upper and lower looper with matching all-purpose or serger thread in the needle. Use heavier decorative thread when serging over thicker fabric such as jersey; use finer thread for serging over lightweight filler.

For a heavier braid, remove the presser foot or use a *Hobbylock* beading foot. For a thinner braid, you may be able to use the standard presser foot. Test for the best results.

1. Adjust for a wide, standard N-length balanced stitch with the lower looper slightly tightened.

2. Pull the fabric strip slightly so that it rolls into a tube. Place the tube between the needle and the knife. If you are using a presser foot, put the tube under the back and over the front of the foot (or in the beading foot guides). Allow approximately an inch of the tube to extend in back of the foot.

3. Hold the end of the tube taut behind the foot to prevent jamming as you begin to serge. If you are not using a foot, carefully guide the taut tube between the needle and knife as you serge.

4. Continue to hold the serged braid taut (but **don't** pull), guiding it smoothly out behind the foot or needle. The stitches should form around, and not through, the tube. (Fig. 5-56)

Puffed serged braid may be hand-tacked to your fabric to form a letter

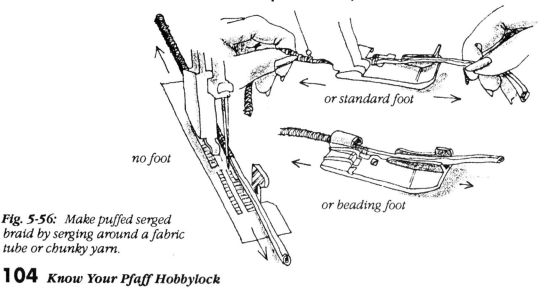

or standard foot

no foot

or beading foot

Fig. 5-56: *Make puffed serged braid by serging around a fabric tube or chunky yarn.*

or design. Twist or braid strands together for a more pronounced trim. (Fig. 5-57)

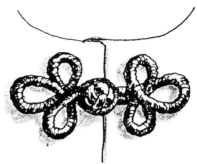

Fig. 5-58: Make your own decorative frog closures with puffed serged braid.

Fig. 5-57: Puffed serged braid can be tacked or fused to fabric to form letters or designs. Twist or braid multiple strands for a pronounced effect.

S **Special Tip:** Use fusible thread in the lower looper to create fusible puffed braid. In most instances, the fusible thread will permanently bond the braid in place. For more durability, hand-tack the braid to the fabric, catching only the under side of the braid.

Project: Frog Closures

Heavy rayon thread is serged over a tube of wool jersey, then easily formed into traditional frog closures. Use two on the fringed scarf in Lesson 26 (page 124) or embellish your latest fashion garment. (Fig. 5-58)

Foot: None
Stitch: 3-thread
Stitch length: Standard N
Stitch width: Widest

Thread: Matching color
  Needle: All-purpose or serger
  Upper looper: Heavy rayon, like *Decor 6* or pearl rayon
  Lower looper: Woolly nylon
Tension: Balanced, with lower looper slightly tightened
Needle: Size 11/75
Fabric: Two 1" strips of 60"-wide wool or acrylic jersey, cut on the crosswise grain

1. Create puffed braid from the 60" jersey strips, following the instructions on page 103.

2. Cut two 10-1/2" strips and two 22" strips of the braid. Apply seam sealant to each end and allow it to dry.

3. From the short strips, form decorative loops, as shown. (Fig. 5-59) Hand-tack the braid together from the wrong side.

Fig. 5-59: Form the looped side of the closure and hand-tack the ends.

4. Using the longer strips, make a button with decorative loops matching those in step 3. (Fig. 5-60) Hand-tack the braid together from the wrong side.

Fig. 5-60: *Make a ball button, then form the tail into three decorative loops.*

Lesson 21.
Serged Picot Braid

Create a delicate but stable picot braid by serging on water-soluble stabilizer. Using a heavy decorative thread in the upper looper and monofilament nylon thread in the lower looper creates the appearance of a looped single strand. After zig-zagging along the needleline and washing away the stabilizer, the braid may be glued to an accessory or craft project or top-stitched to a feminine blouse or dress.

Single-picot braid

1. Thread your serger with pearl cotton or crochet thread in the upper looper, monofilament nylon in the lower looper, and all-purpose or serger thread in the needle. Adjust for the longest, widest, balanced 3-thread stitch. For maximum width, try removing the upper looper thread from the tension disc (see page 25).

2. Serge-finish a strip of water-soluble stabilizer. (For a long strand of braid, cut more than one stabilizer strip and lap the short ends during serging to reach the length desired.) To secure the serging, zigzag over the needleline with a narrow stitch and matching thread. (Fig. 5-61)

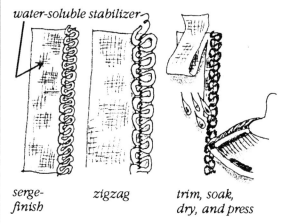

water-soluble stabilizer

serge-finish · · · zigzag · · · trim, soak, dry, and press

Fig. 5-61: *To make picot braid, serge-finish water-soluble stabilizer. Zigzag over the needleline, trim the excess stabilizer, and soak the braid before drying and pressing.*

3. Trim the stabilizer about 1/8" from the serging.

4. Soak the braid in cold or luke-warm water, then lay it flat on a paper towel to dry. Or blot the braid with a paper towel to remove most of the moisture and dry it in a microwave oven on a medium power setting for approximately two minutes. (For safety, set the timer for one-minute intervals or less and check after each period.) Make sure the braid is as flat as possible while drying. When dry, press the braid flat using a press cloth.

Double-picot braid

Two rows of single-picot stitches combine to form a wider, double picot braid.

1. Complete steps 1 and 2 for single-picot braid.

2. Turn the strip in the opposite direction and serge a second row with the needleline right next to or on top of the first needleline. (You will be trimming off all the excess stabilizer as you serge this second row.) (Fig. 5-62)

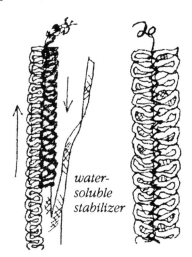

Fig. 5-62: Serge double-picot braid by overlapping the needlelines of two single-picot rows. Then zigzag over the needlelines before washing out the stabilizer.

3. To stabilize the braid, zigzag the needlelines together with a narrow stitch and matching thread.

4. Finish by following step 4 for single picot braid.

Picot-braid variations

■ Use finer thread and a shorter stitch for a fluffier effect. Test the finer decorative thread in both loopers for a thicker braid.

■ Try various length, width, and tension settings, as well as different thread types and combinations.

■ For fusible picot braid, use fusible thread in the bobbin of the zigzag stitch. Using a press cloth, fuse the braid in place on the garment or project.

■ Save a step by zigzagging the braid to a washable project or garment fabric during step 3 of both the single- and double-picot braids. Then moisten or wash the entire piece to remove the excess stabilizer.

Stretch picot braid

Add stretch to your picot braid by serging it over transparent elastic as well as water-soluble stabilizer. This decorative, elasticized braid is perfect for hiding stitched hems and edges on swimsuits and exercisewear.

1. Complete step 1 for single picot braid.

2. Position 1/4"-wide transparent elastic over a 1"-wide strip of water-soluble stabilizer. Serge over both layers, just catching the needle in the edge of the elastic and stretching the elastic slightly as you serge. (Fig. 5-63)

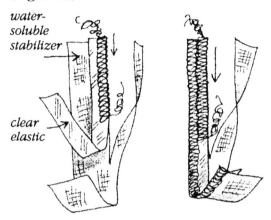

water-soluble stabilizer

clear elastic

Fig. 5-63: *Serge stretch picot braid over clear elastic and water-soluble stabilizer. Overlap needlelines on the second row.*

3. After serging one side, turn the braid around and serge the other side with the needle next to the needleline of the previous stitching. Rinse out the stabilizer and allow the strip to dry.

4. Secure the braid to a stretch-fabric garment using a narrow zigzag stitch over the braid needlelines.

Project: Picot-trimmed Hat

Picot-braid flowers transform a plain summer hat into a fashion statement. (Fig. 5-64)

Foot: Standard
Stitch: 3-thread
Stitch length: Longest
Stitch width: Widest

Fig. 5-64: *Picot braid flowers highlight a summer hat.*

Thread: Contrasting color to hat
  Needle: All-purpose or serger
  Upper looper: Pearl cotton or crochet thread
  Lower looper: Monofilament nylon
Tension: Balanced
Needle: Size 11/75
Notions: One hat with large brim; 6" by 27" piece of water-soluble stabilizer; clear-drying fabric glue

Note: Each flower will use approximately 2/3 yard of braid. Serge four yards of braid for four flowers and select the best lengths for your project.

1. Thread and adjust your serger for picot braid following the instructions on page 106. Serge-finish one long edge of the stabilizer.

2. Zigzag over the needleline with a narrow stitch and matching thread.

3. Trim the stabilizer about 1/8" from the serging.

4. Soak the braid to remove the stabilizer. Then dry and press the braid.

5. Repeat steps 1 through 4 until you have enough yardage for your project.

6. Use a water-soluble marker to draw flower placement outlines on the hat.

7. Glue the picot braid onto the outlines, starting and ending in the center of each flower.

Lesson 22. Serged Couching Braid

In Lesson 20 (page 103), we featured puffed serged braid—one of our favorites for couched monograms and other designs. Another of our favorite couching braids is serged using a base of water-soluble stabilizer. It is flat and wider than puffed serged braid and, after moistening to remove the stabilizer, can be accurately pre-shaped into any design and dried before couching it to the fabric.

1. Adjust for the widest, satin-length, balanced 3-thread stitch with pearl cotton (or other similar heavy thread) in both loopers and all-purpose or serger thread in the needle.

 Note: Remember that the thread used for this braid must be washable because it will be moistened to remove the stabilizer.

2. Serge-finish a strip of water-soluble stabilizer, then turn the strip in the opposite direction and serge a second row with the needleline on top of or to the left of the first needleline. (You will be trimming off all the excess stabilizer as you serge this second row.) (Fig. 5-65) For a

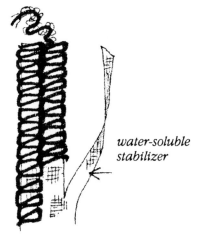

water-soluble stabilizer

Fig. 5-65: *Serge two rows of couching braid, overlapping the needlelines.*

long strand of braid, cut more than one stabilizer strip and lap the short ends during serging to reach the length desired.

3. If you want to make a wider couching braid, serge again along one or both sides of the braid, with the needle inside the loops of one of the original rows.

4. Gently stretch the serged braid to set the stitches—it will be lengthened and narrowed. (On longer braid sections, start at the end and carefully slide the stitches along the needleline when stretching.) Then moisten the braid to remove the excess stabilizer and shape the braid into any design

Fig. 5-66: *After stretching and moistening, shape the braid into a letter or design, then let dry.*

before drying. (Fig. 5-66) Because the dried braid holds its shape well, it's easy to create any letter or shape, including mirror-image designs for couching onto opposite sides of a garment.

5. Tuck under both unfinished, narrow ends of the braid before top-stitching it to your garment or project.

Project: Monogrammed Hand Towel

Turn a simple towel into a treasured keepsake by applying serged couching braid. (Fig. 5-67)

Fig. 5-67: *Easily monogram towels for special gifts, using serged couching braid.*

Foot: Standard
Stitch: 3-thread
Stitch length: Satin
Stitch width: Widest
Thread: Contrasting
    Needle: All-purpose or serger
    Upper looper: Heavy decorative (washable) such as pearl cotton
    Lower looper: Heavy decorative (washable) such as pearl cotton
Tension: Balanced
Needle: Size 14/90
Notions: One terry hand towel; one strip water-soluble stabilizer, the length of the serged couching braid; small piece of white freezer paper

1. Determine the letter or letters you'll be monogramming and draw them (or trace them from a pattern or stencil) onto white freezer paper to make a pattern. Measure the distance to be monogrammed.

2. Serge a double row of couching braid over the water-soluble stabilizer following the previous instructions. Make enough to cover the monogram.

3. Starting from the front end of the braid, gently stretch it. Then moisten it, blot out the excess water, and shape it on top of the pattern.

4. After drying, place the monogram on the hand towel, tucking the ends under and top-stitching around all edges.

6. *Special Decorative Serging Techniques*

- Lesson 23. Gathering and Shirring
- Lesson 24. Serger Lace
- Lesson 25. Decorative Flatlocking
- Lesson 26. Fringing
- Lesson 27. Serging over Trim
- Lesson 28. Sequin, Bead, and Pearl Application
- Lesson 29. Serge-Couching

In past lessons you've mastered seams, edges, bindings, braids, and other trims. Now it's time to explore some of the special decorative techniques that make serger sewing so much fun. You can embellish fabric with flatlocking, trims, beading, and couching. You can gather, shirr, and fringe. You can even make a delicate, tatting-like lace with serger stitches.

Although decoratively serging seams and edges can ornament your lastest fashion garments in high style, many more options are available as well. By serging along folds, you can add embellishment anywhere on your fabric. Practically any decorative technique you see in ready-to-wear can be duplicated.

The lessons in this chapter will lead you through some of our favorite serger applications. You'll be delighted with the number of additional ornamental serging possibilities they open up for you.

Lesson 23. Gathering and Shirring

We use several different methods of serge-gathering to create ruffles, attach full skirts to waistbands or bodices, and to ornament other serger projects. Although generally fast and easy, serge-gathering works best on projects that do not require the wider seam allowances used for couture tailoring or delicate fabrics.

The width of the serge-gathered seam allowance is limited by the width of the serged stitch. The weight or thickness of your fabric and the project itself help determine what method to use. With serge-gathering, a single layer of fabric will gather more than multiple layers.

Tension gathering

For easy gathering of lightweight fabric, tighten the needle tension almost all the way. Use a long stitch, your widest width, and a balanced 3-thread stitch. If you are using two needles, tighten both needle tensions. Vary the amount of gathers by changing the stitch length. A longer stitch length will gather the fabric more.

For speedier tension gathering, instead of tightening the tension controls, press the needle thread(s) against the face of your serger below the needle tension controls, as shown. (Fig. 6-1) This instant finger tensioning returns to normal just by releasing the threads.

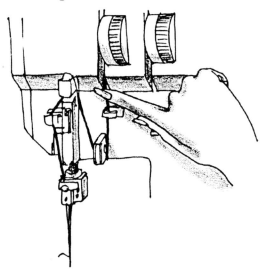

Fig. 6-1: *To quickly gather lightweight fabric, apply tension to the needle thread.*

Differential-feed gathering

If your serger has differential feed, you can use it to easily gather lightweight fabrics. Use a wide, standard N-length, and balanced stitch. Adjust the differential feed to 2.0 for serge-gathering. To vary the amount of gathers, change the differential-feed setting or the length of the stitch.

To softly gather or ease only one layer when you are serging two layers, lengthen the stitch. With the differential feed on 2.0, hold the top layer taut. On light- to medium-weight fabrics, the under layer will gather as you serge it to the top layer. Softer fabrics will gather more than stiff fabrics. Shorten your stitch length to reduce the amount of gathering.

Filler-cord gathering

To serge-gather medium- to heavy-weight fabrics, serge over a strand of filler thread such as buttonhole twist, crochet thread, or pearl cotton. (Fig. 6-2) Use a wide, standard N-length

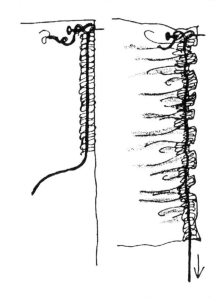

Fig. 6-2: *For medium- to heavy-weight fabric, serge over filler cord and pull to gather.*

(or shorter), and balanced 3- or 3/4-thread stitch. Place the filler under the back and over the front of the presser foot (or use a beading or ribbon foot), guiding it with the techniques from Lesson 4 (page 49). Serge over the filler, being careful not to cut it. Secure one end of the filler and pull the other end to gather the edge.

If your serger has a 3/4-thread stitch, you can use both needles as you serge. Guide the filler between the needles. (Fig. 6-3) The needle threads hold the filler in position for more controlled gathering.

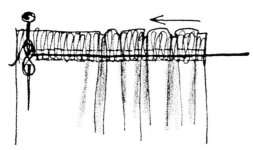

Fig. 6-3: *For more controlled gathering, place the filler thread between the two needles of a 3/4-thread stitch.*

 Special Tip: Use the ribbon foot for the easiest guiding of the filler thread between the two needles. Test first on scraps for accurate filler-cord alignment.

Thread-chain gathering

This technique uses thread chain as a gathering filler cord. Serge off a thread chain that is slightly longer than the edge to be gathered. Raise the presser foot and bring the chain under the back and over the front of the foot (or use the beading or ribbon foot). Insert the fabric under the foot and serge over the chain, using a 3-thread stitch, as if you were using filler thread. Then draw the chain up to gather. Or hold the chain taut to gather as your serge.

Serge-shirring

Parallel rows of serge-shirring can create a stretchy waistband or cuffs on your latest fashion garments. We prefer to shirr the fabric first, before cutting it out. In addition to gathering in the fabric lengthwise, the serge-shirred stitching takes up extra fabric width—about twice the width of the serged stitch for each row of shirring.

For easiest serge-shirring, begin with a long strip of elastic thread, cording, or narrow clear elastic. (For more durability when shirring with elastic thread, serge over two or more strands.) Mark the desired length of your finished shirring on the elastic using a marking pen, leaving some extra at the beginning end. After serge-shirring over the elastic and fabric (see the instructions following), secure the unmarked end of elastic by pinning or sewing it and gather it from the opposite end. (Fig. 6-4) Because

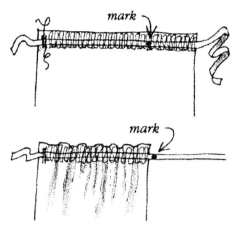

mark

mark

Fig. 6-4: *Shirr accurately by marking the desired length on the elastic. Serge over the elastic, secure one end, and gather to the mark.*

you've serged over the elastic, not into it, it will pull easily. When the mark is exposed, secure and trim that end of the elastic and adjust the shirring evenly.

To serge-shirr using *elastic thread or cording,* adjust your serger for a standard N-width, standard N-length, and balanced 3-thread stitch. To serge-shirr with 1/8" *clear elastic,* use a wide stitch instead. Place the elastic under the back and over the front of the presser foot (or use a beading or ribbon foot) as for the filler-cord gathering on page 112.

To begin, serge several stitches over the elastic until you reach the beginning mark you made. Fold the fabric right sides together and place it under the presser foot. Serge over the

folded edge, being careful not to cut the fabric or elastic. Secure one end of the elastic by pinning or sewing it, then pull up the elastic to complete the shirring.

For more controlled shirring, serge over elastic thread using a 3/4-thread stitch. Feed the elastic thread between the two needles, as for the 3/4-thread filler cord application (see page 113). The shirring will be a little bulkier and will require more fabric because of the wider stitch, but it will remain more evenly distributed during wearing.

An optional shirring method is to serge through a strip of wider clear elastic, stretching the elastic as you serge. Use 1/4- or 3/8"-wide clear elastic. Adjust your serger for a standard N stitch width and long stitch length. Thread the elastic under the back and over the front of the foot or use the ribbon or elastic foot for easier guiding. Evenly section and mark the elastic and the fabric, leaving a section for starting before the first mark on the elastic. Serge a few stitches on the elastic, then insert the folded fabric at the first mark. Serge, stretching the elastic to match the section marks, as shown. (Fig. 6-5)

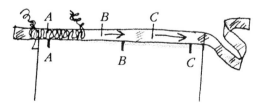

Fig. 6-5: *Shirr while serging by stretching clear elastic to meet presectioned markings.*

Special Tip: When using the elastic foot, thread the elastic through the foot and out and under the back before attaching the foot to the machine. Before shirring your project, test the foot adjustment on a project scrap until you reach the desired amount of stretch.

Double chainstitch shirring

Serge-shirring may also be done using the 2-thread double chainstitch on the 797 model. Thread elastic cording in the chain looper and adjust for a long stitch. Loosen both the needle and looper thread tensions slightly. Serge rows of shirring, using the presser foot to guide the width of the rows. For ease in handling multiple rows of serge-shirring, serge them over a strip of adding-machine tape or freezer paper. Tear away the paper after serging.

Project: Shirred Ponytail Tube

This simple yet pretty hair ornament is gathered with serge-shirred elastic. Rolled-edge stitching adds a decorative finish. Vary the fabric and measurements to whip up tubes and headbands for any occasion. (Fig. 6-6)

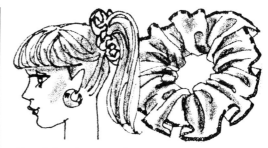

Fig. 6-6: *Shirred tubes dress up a hairstyle for special occasions or every day.*

Foot: Standard, ribbon, or elastic for elastic application; rolled edge for finishing
Stitch: 3-thread
Stitch length: Standard N for elastic application; short for rolled edge
Stitch width: Standard N for elastic application; narrow for rolled edge
Thread: Matching or contrasting color
Needle: All-purpose or serger
Upper looper: All-purpose or serger for elastic application; decorative for rolled edge
Lower looper: All-purpose or serger
Tension: Balanced for elastic application; rolled edge for finishing
Needle: Size 11/75
Fabric: One strip 3-1/2" wide by 18" long
Notions: 24" of elastic cording or 1-1/3 yards of elastic thread (used double-strand)

1. Allowing a 2" tail, thread the elastic under the back and over the front of the presser foot, or use a ribbon or elastic foot (see page 113 for more details). Serge several stitches over the elastic with a standard N-width, balanced stitch.

2. Fold the fabric strip right sides together. Serge over the elastic on the folded fabric edge, being careful not to cut the fabric or elastic.

3. Secure one end of the elastic. Pull the opposite end to gather the fabric (to about 6" to 7" finished).

4. With the fabric ends flat and with the right sides of both ends together, straight-stitch the ends into a tube, back-stitching over the elastic to secure. (Fig. 6-7) Knot the elastic ends and trim.

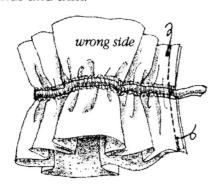

Fig. 6-7: After pulling the elastic to shirr, straight-stitch the ends to form a tube. Back-stitch over the elastic to secure.

5. Fold the fabric wrong sides together. Finish the tube by serge-seaming with a rolled edge, overlapping the beginning stitching to finish.

Lesson 24. Serger Lace

One of our favorite details for finishing dainty tucks on garment fronts and collars, serger lace also has interesting applications on numerous craft and accessory projects.

This lace is made by merely overlapping rows of balanced 3-thread serging. The appearance of serger lace can be varied by the thread used in the loopers and the number of rows of serging (more rows create a wider lace). Using buttonhole twist will give the look of a hand-crocheted edge. Lightweight thread creates a more delicate effect.

1. Adjust your serger for the longest, widest 3-thread stitch. You may need to loosen the needle tension slightly.

2. Serge one row of stitching to the fabric, allowing all but the needleline to hang off the edge. Leave at least a 4" thread chain at each end.

3. Overlap a second row of serging with the needle inside the overlocking loops of the first row of stitching. (Fig. 6-8) For accuracy, align the

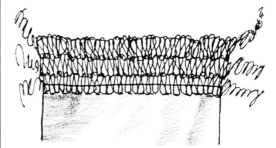

Fig. 6-8: Overlap rows of 3-thread serging to form lace.

loops with the raised ledge on the presser foot when adding the additional row.

4. To make wider lace, continue overlapping rows of serging to the width desired. It may take a little practice to position the needle just inside the loops. If the needle misses stitching inside the loops, you will have a hole in the lace. In this case, simply find the shortest thread (the needle thread) and pull it. The loops will fall away from the previous stitching, and you can serge the row again.

5. To widen the lace after serging, gently pull it crosswise, away from the fabric. If you want to ruffle the lace, gently stretch it parallel to the edge. (Fig. 6-9)

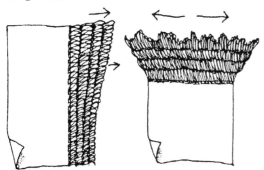

Fig. 6-9: *Gently pull the lace crosswise to widen it. Stretch it parallel to the edge to ruffle it.*

Stabilized lace

Make a perfect serged lace edge with water-soluble stabilizer as a base.

1. Serge-finish the fabric edge.

2. Cut a piece of stabilizer four times the finished width by the finished length of the lace you'll be making.

3. Adjust your serger for the longest, widest, and balanced 3-thread stitch.

4. Place the stabilizer on the wrong side of the finished fabric, allowing it to extend 1/4" beyond the edge. Serge with the needleline just inside the loops of the previous stitching. (Fig. 6-10)

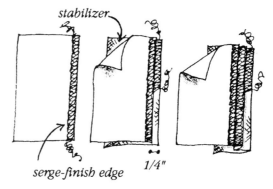

Fig. 6-10: *Add stabilized lace to a fabric edge. Serge-finish the edge. Place water-soluble stabilizer underneath, extending 1/4" beyond the edge. Serge, catching the needleline inside the previous stitching. Fold the stabilizer and repeat for the desired width. Spray or soak to remove the stabilizer.*

5. Fold the stabilizer to the right of the serging. Then refold the stabilizer back, leaving a stitch width of stabilizer to the right of the stitching, as shown.

6. Serge over the fold with the needleline just inside the loops of the previous stitching. Repeat for each additional row until the lace is the desired width.

7. Carefully spray the lace or soak it in water to remove the stabilizer. Allow the lace to air dry or dry it in the microwave on medium power, setting the timer for one-minute intervals and checking after each minute. When dry, it will have a starched feel. To soften it, carefully manipulate the lace with your fingers.

Make a stable lace trim following the same procedure. Begin by cutting the stabilizer following step 2 on page 117 and adjusting your serger following step 3. Serge-finish one long edge of the stabilizer, then follow steps 5 through 7 to complete the trim. (Fig. 6-11)

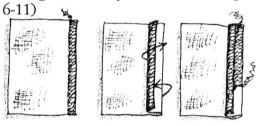

Fig. 6-11: Make stable lace trim by serging one edge of the stabilizer, folding it to the right and refolding to leave a stitch-width to the right. Serge the new fold with the needle just inside the previous stitch. Repeat for the width desired.

Serger lace tucks

Serger lace tucks are easier if you serge onto the fabric before cutting out the project. Begin by folding the fabric on the first tuck line. Serge-finish the edge with the needle about 1/8" inside the fold. Allow the loops to hang off the edge of the fabric. (Use a blindhem foot to ensure even stitching.) Continue folding and serging the tucks, using the presser foot to guide your stitching evenly. (Fig. 6-12) For wider lace tucks, serge

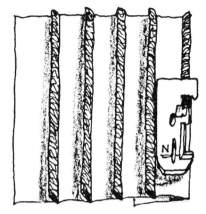

Fig. 6-12: Serge even lace tucks by guiding the presser-foot edge along the previous row.

another row of stitching inside the first row of loops. Delicate care may be required for this wider lace.

Lacy fishline ruffles

To add a lace finish on the edge of fishline ruffles, apply the fishline according to the instructions in Lesson 6 (page 61). Serge the first row of lace with the needle just inside the rolled edge. Serge additional rows for wider lace.

Lace-trimmed wires

Serger lace also can be used to trim fine, flexible wires for craft projects. Cover the wire with a narrow rolled-edge stitch. For the easiest application, use the beading foot (see Lesson 7, page 63). Or guide the wire under the presser foot between the needle and the knife, **serging slowly.**

Change to the standard foot and adjust your serger for a wide, long, and balanced 3-thread stitch. Place the covered wire under the back and over the front of the presser foot, next to the raised ledge on the foot. Or place the wire under the foot, carefully aligning it with the ledge. Serge over the covered wire with the stitch loops hanging off the edge.

Serge additional rows to make wider lace. Shape the lace-trimmed wire as desired and twist the ends together. (Fig. 6-13) Secure all the thread ends with seam sealant.

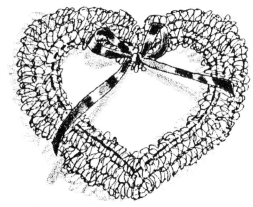

Fig. 6-13: *Serge lace over covered wire and shape as desired.*

Project:
Serger-Lace Flower

Make a delicate flower by adding rows of serger lace to a strip of bias tricot. After serge-gathering, apply stiffening agent to the flower to keep it looking fresh and fluffy. Vary the size of the flower or the type of thread used. Attach your finished sample to the padded picture frame completed in Lesson 16 (page 96). (Fig. 6-14)

Fig. 6-14: *Make a delicate flower by gathering serger lace.*

Foot: Standard
Stitch: 3-thread
Stitch length: Long
Stitch width: Widest
Thread:
   Needle: All-purpose or serger
   Upper looper: All-purpose or
      serger
   Lower looper: All-purpose or
      serger
Tension: Balanced
Needle: Size 11/75
Notions: 18" of 5/8"-wide *Seams Great* or other bias tricot; stiffening spray or dip, such as *Stiffy* or *TAC Spray Stiff*

1. Apply serger lace to one long edge of the bias tricot, following the previous instructions. Begin with one row of stitching on the tricot, then add four more rows of stitching to complete the lace. (Fig. 6-15)

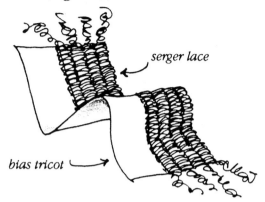

Fig. 6-15: *Serge four rows of lace on the edge of an 18" tricot strip.*

2. Serge-gather the unfinished side of the tricot using the tension or differential-feed methods in Lesson 23 (pages 111-112). If the edge does not gather tightly, pull the needle thread (the shortest thread) to gather it further.

3. Spray (or dip) the flower with stiffening solution, following the directions on the bottle.

4. Glue or hand-tack the finished flower to the padded picture frame, covering the joined ends of the piped binding.

Lesson 25. Decorative Flatlocking

In Lesson 3, we discussed basic flatlocking as it relates to flatlocked seams. Flatlocking also can be applied on folds, so it can be used as decorative detailing anywhere on a garment or project. Among its varied applications, flatlocking can be stitched at angles across the front of an embellished sweatshirt or added as a delicate accent on dressier cuffs and collars.

For the following techniques, unless otherwise specified, adjust your serger for basic flatlocking tensions. (See page 44 for details.) Loosen the needle tension enough to allow the serging to pull flat after being stitched. Tighten the lower looper until it forms a straight line, and use decorative thread in the upper looper.

For most flatlocking, simply move the fabric fold to the left of the knife about half of the stitch width. This also allows the stitches to hang off the edge for the flattest flatlocking. Use the blindhem foot to stitch accurately. Place the fold of the fabric against the foot's guide, and adjust the guide so that the fold is positioned in the center of the stitching.

In addition to balanced 3-thread flatlocking, other novelty flatlocking effects can be achieved by changing tensions, stitch widths, and thread types.

Corded flatlocking

Flatlocking does not always require a wide stitch width. Narrow, satin-stitch flatlocking gives the appearance of cording or piping. For a more corded effect, use the right needle (on a 3/4-thread machine) and tighten the needle tension slightly to raise the

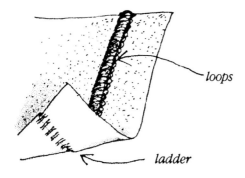

Fig. 6-16: *For corded flatlocking, tighten the needle tension.*

stitch. (Fig. 6-16) Shorten the stitch length for maximum thread coverage. A narrow ladder stitch will show from the underside. For the narrowest corded flatlocking, use the rolled-edge foot.

Safety-stitch flatlocking

Flatlock with a wide 3/4-thread stitch for safety-stitched flatlocking. Use a short- to standard N-length, wide stitch and loosen both needle tensions. (Fig. 6-17) On the under-

side, the ladder stitch will look just like the 3-thread flatlock. The loops on the top side will have an extra right needle-thread line showing. For accuracy, use the blindhem foot as a guide. Adjust to the widest setting, making sure both needles are serging on the fabric.

Safety-stitch flatlocking may not pull completely flat if you are unable to loosen your needle tensions enough. An option for this stitch is to create a raised fold underneath the flatlocked loops using a slightly tighter needle tension. (Fig. 6-17)

Balanced flatlocking

Basic 3-thread flatlocking can be adjusted so the looper tensions are balanced, with the upper and lower looper stitches overlocking in the center of the stitch. (Fig. 6-18)

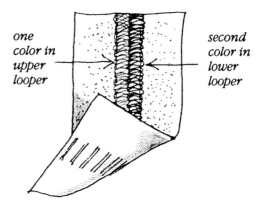

Fig. 6-18: *Flatlocking with balanced looper tensions creates a two-toned stitch.*

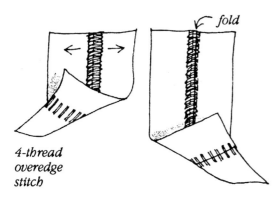

Fig. 6-17: *Loosen both needle tensions for safety-stitch flatlocking. With slightly tighter tension, a fold forms underneath the loops.*

Adjust for 3-thread flatlocking, then tighten the upper looper tension and loosen the lower looper tension. The needle tension remains loose so the stitch will lie flat. Use contrasting thread colors in the loopers for a multicolored stitch.

Mock hemstitching

For mock hemstitching, simply straight-stitch through a wide flatlocked stitch. For the ladder side out, flatlock with the right sides together. Pull the fabric flat. Top-stitch from the wrong side with monofilament nylon thread in the bobbin and thread that matches the fabric in the needle. (Fig. 6-19) The

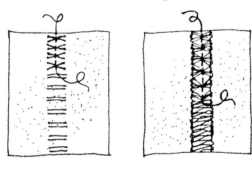

ladder on right side   *loops on right side*

Fig. 6-19: *Straight-stitch either the looped or ladder side of the flatlocking to create mock hemstitching.*

ladder stitches will automatically bunch together. With this stitch, the serger needle thread is the ladder thread that shows, so the decorative thread you use must be able to be threaded through the needle. Experiment with the stitch length for different effects.

Mock hemstitching also can be flatlocked with the looped side out. (Fig. 6-19) Use the decorative thread in the looper. Flatlock and then top-stitch from the ladder side with monofilament nylon thread in the bobbin and thread that matches the fabric in the needle.

Serge-fagoting

Fagoting is a decorative flatlock stitch used for fabric embellishment or seams when the area will not be subjected to much stress, such as the front of a blouse. Most often used in heirloom sewing on fine fabrics, fagoting is serged with the ladder side out. Use decorative thread in the needle. For inconspicuous loops (they may be seen from the top side after the edges are pulled apart), use monofilament nylon thread in the upper looper.

If you apply serge-fagoting to your garment fabric before cutting it out, establish a fagoting seamline and cut along it. Serge-finish the seam allowances and press them to the wrong side. Adjust for a long, wide flatlock stitch. With right sides together and the folds aligned, flatlock with the needle barely catching the edge of the

Fig. 6-20: *For serge-fagoting, press back the seam allowances. Flatlock, barely catching the folds. Then pull the stitches flat.*

Fig. 6-21: *Display decorative flatlocking options on a pretty pin cushion.*

fabric. Pull the stitching flat and press carefully. (Fig. 6-20)

For further embellishment, thread 1/8"-wide ribbon through the ladder stitches. Securely top-stitch the seam allowances on both sides of the fagoting, using a decorative stitch on your sewing machine or the 2-thread double chainstitch on the 797 model. Then center your pattern over the yardage and cut it out.

Project:
Sampler Pin Cushion

Practice these new techniques by making rows of decorative flatlocking on this handy pin cushion. Select a soft woven fabric and tone-on-tone thread for a subtle effect. (Fig. 6-21)

Foot: Blindhem or standard
Stitch: 3- and 3/4-thread
Stitch length: Short for corded flatlocking, balanced flatlocking, and mock hemstitching; standard N for safety-stitch; and long for fagoting
Stitch width: Narrow for corded; widest for all others
Thread: Same tone as fabric; monofilament nylon for bobbin
Needle(s): All-purpose, serger, or rayon
Upper looper: All-purpose, serger, or rayon
Lower looper: All-purpose or serger; contrasting tone for balanced
Tension: Flatlock, unless otherwise indicated
Needle(s): Size 11/75
Fabric: 1/4 yard batiste, organdy, or broadcloth
Notions: 1/3 yard of 1/8"-wide satin ribbon—same tone as fabric and thread; polyester fiberfill for stuffing

1. Cut one 9" square from the fabric. Cut the square in half on the lengthwise grain.

2. On one long side of each piece, press 1/2" to the wrong side. With right sides together, apply fagoting. Pull the piece flat and weave the ribbon through the fagoted stitch. Decoratively top-stitch or chainstitch on both sides of the fagoting.

3. On both sides of the fagoting, with right sides together, serge a row of mock hemstitching a presser foot's width away from the fagoting. Top-stitch from the wrong side with monofilament nylon in the bobbin.

4. Serge a row of balanced flatlocking on either side of the mock hemstitching, using a contrasting thread color in the lower looper. Use the presser-foot width as a stitching guide.

5. On either side of the balanced flatlocking, serge a row of narrow corded flatlocking. Then, if your serger has a 3/4-thread stitch, add rows of safety-stitch flatlocking.

6. Cut one 6" by 7" rectangle from the flatlocked fabric and two 6" by 7" rectangles from the unfinished fabric.

7. Using one of the plain rectangles as a backing for the flatlocked piece, place the right sides of the rectangles together. Serge-seam with a wide, standard N-length, and balanced 3- or 3/4-thread stitch. Leave an opening on one side to stuff the fiberfill.

8. Stuff the pin cushion and hand-tack the opening closed.

Lesson 26. Fringing

We see fringing on everything from scarves and garment edges to tablecloths and napkins. Using either flatlocking or balanced stitching, you can add a stable, decorative accent to the edge of any fringe. For fastest fringing, choose a fabric that ravels easily.

Flatlocked fringe

Choose balanced flatlocking or one of the other flatlocking options in Lesson 25.

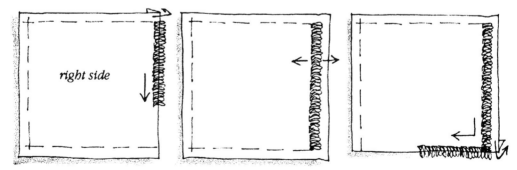

Fig. 6-22: *For flatlocked fringe, serge on the fold between the intersecting lines. Pull the stitching flat, turn the square corner, and repeat for the adjoining side.*

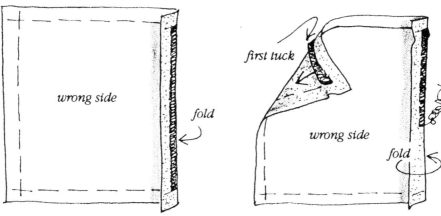

Fig. 6-23: *For tucked fringe, use a balanced stitch. Serge between the intersecting marks and fold the tuck toward the center. Repeat for the adjoining sides.*

1. Select the width of fringe desired and pull a thread to mark the lines—at least 1" from the edge.

2. Fold your fabric wrong sides together and flatlock over the fringe line with a short- to standard N-length, standard N-width stitch. Use a matching or contrasting thread color in both the upper looper and the needle.

3. Start at a corner where the marked lines intersect. Flatlock to the next intersection and (before turning) pull the previous stitching flat. (Fig. 6-22) Fold the next side, turn the fabric a quarter turn, and repeat for the remaining sides.

4. Secure the ends by weaving the thread chains under the stitching.

5. For easiest fringing, clip from the cut edge to (but not through) the stitching every 2". Fringe to the stitching line by pulling out the horizontal threads.

Tucked fringe

For this edging option, serge a tuck and then top-stitch it down to the fabric, next to the area to be fringed.

1. Put decorative thread in the upper looper and adjust for a short, standard N or wider, balanced 3-thread stitch.

2. Pull a thread 1-1/4" away from the edges to mark the fringing lines.

3. Fold under 1-1/4" to the wrong side and, with the wrong side up, serge-finish along the fold to form a tuck. At the corner, serge to the intersection of the marked lines. Raise the presser foot, clear the stitches from the stitch finger, pull the fabric back behind the needle, and serge off. (Fig. 6-23)

4. Fold the serge-finished tuck away from the cut edge. Fold the adjoining edge along the marked line, in the same manner as for step 3. Clear the stitches from the stitch finger again and position the needle directly over the outside edge of the previous stitching. Begin by serging over the previous tuck, then continue serging the edge as in step 3.

5. Repeat steps 3 and 4 for the remaining edges to be fringed.

6. Press the finished tucks away from the edges. Hide the thread chains under the tucks and top-stitch to secure.

7. Clip the cut edges below the tucks every 2" and fringe by pulling out the horizontal threads.

Project: Fringed Triangle Scarf

This fashionable scarf is made from a folded square of challis. The double thickness gives a thick fringed edge, and the bias fold drapes softly at the neckline. Attach the corded frog closures made in Lesson 20 (page 103). Whether you wear it with the frogs in front or at the shoulder, the scarf will stay securely in place. (Fig. 6-24)

Fig. 6-24: *Fringe two sides of a folded challis triangle. Secure with frog closures from Lesson 20.*

Foot: Standard
Stitch: 3-thread
Stitch length: Standard N
Stitch width: Widest
Thread: Contrasting color
   Needle: All-purpose or serger
   Upper looper: Heavy rayon, such as *Decor 6* or pearl rayon
   Lower looper: All-purpose or serger
Tension: Balanced
Needle: Size 11/75
Fabric: One yard wool challis

1. Cut a 36" square of challis. On two adjoining sides, pull a thread or press-mark the fabric 1-1/4" from each side to mark the fringe lines.

2. Fold the scarf in half diagonally with the two marked fringe lines on top.

3. On one side, along the marked line, fold both layers of the fringe allowance 1-1/4" to the wrong side. Lightly press. Then turn the wrong side up and serge-finish the fold, stopping at the point where the two marked lines intersect. Raise the presser foot, clear the stitch finger, pull the remaining fabric behind the needle, and chain off.

4. Press the serged tuck toward the fabric, wrapping the thread chains underneath. Top-stitch to secure.

5. Repeat steps 3 and 4 for the other fringed side. Begin serge-finishing with the needle positioned exactly on the outer edge of the previous stitching at the point of the scarf. Serge to the end of the fabric and chain off.

6. On the two scarf points adjoining the folded edge, the fringe allowance and serged tuck will extend past the edge of the scarf. Fold the extension back and, to secure it, top-stitch across the tuck stitching. (Fig. 6-25)

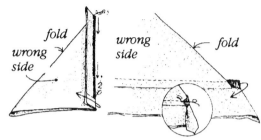

Fig. 6-25: *The fringe and tuck will extend past the folded edge of the scarf. Fold the end under and top-stitch.*

7. Clip the fringe allowance every 2" and pull out the horizontal threads.

8. Hand-tack the frog closures made in Lesson 20 (page 103) to the unfringed scarf edges. Position them 8" and 11" from the bottom of the fringe. Attach the frogs so the edges of the scarf meet, but don't overlap, under the frogs.

Lesson 27.
Serging over Trim

If a decorative thread, yarn, or ribbon is too bulky (or not flexible enough) to thread through your loopers, you have the option of serging over it. To completely cover a trim with serging, the trim must be narrow enough to fit between the needle and the knife. The upper looper also must be able to clear the trim without catching for the stitches to form evenly.

To serge over decorative trim, adjust for a stitch width wide enough to cover the trim. The length of the stitch will depend on how much of the trim you want to expose. Start with a standard N stitch length for testing. Use a balanced 3-thread stitch or a flatlock. Use monofilament nylon or matching all-purpose or serger thread in the upper looper to emphasize the trim.

Place the trim under the back and over the front of the presser foot (or use a beading or ribbon foot), guiding it with the filler-cord techniques from Lesson 4 (page 49). Remember to allow several inches of trim to extend behind the foot for easy starting.

 Special Tip: When using the beading foot to help serge over trim, place the trim along the right edge of the foot so that it rests in the front guide and feeds under the back guide. (Fig. 6-26)

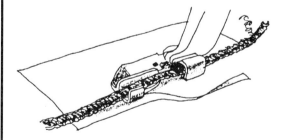

Fig. 6-26: *Serge the trim to the fabric with a beading foot.*

When trimming an edge, bring the fabric completely under the foot to the knife. When flatlocking on a fold, guide the fabric only partially under the foot (away from the knife) so that the trim and stitching will fall half on and half off the fabric; this allows the finished flatlocking to pull flat.

For the easiest feeding, begin serging over the trim for several stitches with no fabric underneath. Then insert the fabric under the foot and serge slowly. Be careful not to stitch through the trim or cut it with the knives. Especially if it's bulky, you may need to hold the trim taut to guide it out from under the back of the foot.

Flatlocking over ribbon

Try flatlocking over a ribbon to cover a seam. The ribbon should be narrow enough to be serged over without cutting or stitching through it. The 1/8"-wide ribbon works with most wide stitch widths. A 1/16"-wide ribbon is also available for a narrower 3-thread stitch.

1. Serge-seam the fabric with right sides together.

2. Apply the ribbon following the instructions for serging over trim on page 127. The ribbon foot (see page 51) is specially designed to position ribbon for the easiest application.

3. Fold the fabric on the seamline, wrong sides together. Raise the presser foot and put the fabric halfway under the ribbon. Flatlock through all layers, with the stitches just covering the ribbon edges. (Fig. 6-27)

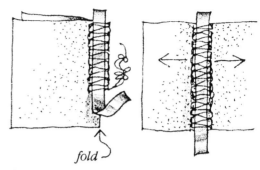

Fig. 6-27: Center ribbon along the fabric fold before flatlocking. The stitches will hang off the edge. Pull flat.

4. Pull the stitching flat and the ribbon will cover the seamline.

Flatlocking over lace and ribbon

Another decorative technique is to center a layer of double-edged lace over the seamline on the right side of the fabric. Then fold the lace and the fabric along the seamline and flatlock the ribbon on top (through all layers) using the previous method for flatlocking over trim and ribbon. (Fig. 6-28)

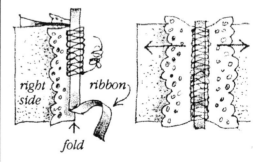

Fig. 6-28: Flatlock to attach a layer of ribbon and lace to fabric.

Flatlocking over yarn

Flatlocking over yarn with mono-filament nylon thread appears to leave the yarn floating on the fabric surface.

1. Fold the fabric right sides together with the yarn inside the fold. (Fig. 6-29)

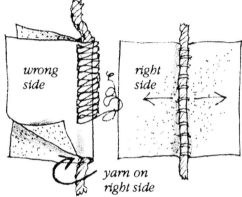

Fig. 6-29: Flatlock over decorative yarn from the wrong side. Only the ladder stitch shows on the right side.

2. Thread monofilament nylon in the needle and matching all-purpose or serger thread in the looper(s).

3. Serge the fold with a wide, long flatlock stitch.

4. Pull the fold flat. From the right side, the yarn floats on the surface, held invisibly by the monofilament.

 Special Tip: If you have difficulty catching the yarn in the fold, baste it with a zigzag stitch to hold it in place for the flatlocking. Use monofilament nylon thread in the needle for invisible zigzag basting.

Project: Heart-shaped Jewelry Holder

This feminine jewelry holder is decoratively finished by flatlocking over ribbon. Covered hooks hold necklaces tangle-free. (Fig. 6-30)

Fig. 6-30: A pillowed jewelry holder keeps bracelets and necklaces tangle-free.

Foot: Ribbon or standard for ribbon application; standard for serge-seaming
Stitch: 3-thread for flatlocking; 3- or 3/4-thread for serge-seaming
Stitch length: Long for flatlocking; standard N for serge-seaming
Stitch width: Widest
Thread: Matching color
   Needle(s): All-purpose or serger
   Upper looper: Monofilament nylon for flatlocking; all-purpose or serger for serge-seaming
   Lower looper: All-purpose or serger

Tension: Flatlocking for ribbon application; balanced for serge-seaming

Needle(s): Size 11/75

Fabric: 1/4 yard batiste; 1/4 yard lace yardage (will make two holders)

Notions: Two yards 1/8"-wide satin ribbon (1/16"-wide for narrower stitch widths); five large covered hooks (used on heavy coats); one yard 3/4"-wide ruffled lace; fiberfill for stuffing

1. Using the pattern grid (Fig. 6-31), cut one lace and two fabric heart pieces.

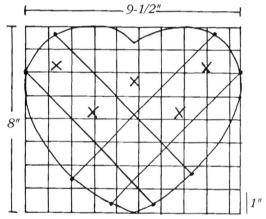

Fig. 6-31: *Jewelry holder pattern, with ribbon and hook placement marked.*

2. Fold the lace heart piece with the wrong sides together and flatlock four strips of ribbon in the positions shown on the pattern grid.

3. Using a standard presser foot, adjust for a balanced stitch. Layer one fabric heart under the lace heart. Fold 1/2" of the ruffled lace to the wrong side. Beginning at the lower point,

place the right side of the ruffled lace against the right side of the two heart layers (lace heart on top). Serge the lace to the heart, pulling the edge to a straight line at the inside corner on the top of the heart. Overlap the beginning lace at the point.

4. With the ruffled lace sandwiched between, place the remaining fabric heart right sides together with the lace heart. Beginning at the lower point, serge-seam, leaving a 3" opening for the stuffing.

5. Turn the heart right side out and stuff with fiberfill. Hand-tack the opening closed.

6. Hand-tack a bow and hanging loop at the top and five hooks on the front, as in the finished view on page 129.

Lesson 28. Sequin, Bead, and Pearl Application

Strands of colorful beads, elegant pearls, and shiny sequins can be serged to edges or anywhere else on your garment or project. Use them for bridalwear, holiday glitz, or just for fun.

Applying beads and pearls

Beaded trims (available at craft and fabric stores or through mail order) can be applied with a flatlock, rolled edge, or even a balanced stitch. The beads must be small enough to fit between the needle and knife and for the upper looper to pass over them.

Purchase enough yardage (at least three extra yards) for thorough testing before application.

Beads or sequins may be applied by removing the presser foot and guiding them manually between the needle and the knife. However, the beading foot simplifies the application for beads or sequins less than 1/4" wide.

1. If your machine has two needles, use the left needle for larger beads and the right needle for smaller beads.

2. Adjust for a stitch slightly longer and wider than the beads you are applying.

3. Use monofilament nylon thread in the upper looper and matching all-purpose or serger thread in the needle and lower looper.

4. If you are attaching the beads to a fold, adjust for a flatlock stitch (see page 44). If you are attaching the beads to an edge, adjust for a rolled edge.

5. Attach the beading foot and place the bead strand along the right side of the foot so that it rests in the front guide and feeds under the back one. Allow 2-3" to extend beyond the back of the foot. (Fig. 6-32)

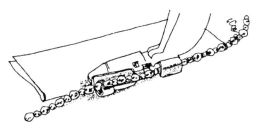

Fig. 6-32: *Easily serge over beaded trim using the beading foot.*

6. Serge slowly over several inches of beading before inserting the fabric. Then guide the fabric fold or edge (bead stitching line) under the front of the foot. Determine how far from the knife you'll guide the fabric during your testing before flatlocking beads to your project.

If you're guiding beads manually without the foot, remember to allow the beads and stitches to hang off the edge when using a flatlock stitch.

To serge off, cut the bead strand and carefully serge over the end. If necessary, use seam sealant to secure the beads before cutting.

 Optional: For a heavier, beaded-crochet trim, use decorative thread in the upper looper. We usually use larger beads and a heavier thread for this application. You must help feed the bead strand (gently) as you serge over it.

Beaded piping

To make a piping strip of beads or pearls, serge the strands to a folded 1-1/4"-wide bias strip of tricot or other lightweight fabric.

Applying sequins

To serge over sequin trim, the sequins must be narrow enough for the looper thread to lock over them. If you are applying them with the beading foot, they need to be less than 1/4" wide (see the previous instructions for applying beads and pearls). Place the trim so that the sequins overlap away from the presser

Fig. 6-33: Overlap sequin trim away from the presser foot.

Fig. 6-34: Beaded trim dresses up the edges of an organza flower.

foot. (Fig. 6-33) Serge over the sequin strand with a long stitch, being careful to avoid hitting the needle or knife. Use monofilament nylon thread or matching thread in the upper looper. After serging, slip the upper looper threads between the sequins so no thread is visible.

Project: Bead-edged Flower

A strand of pearl beading can be applied to a folded edge of organza to create an elegant flower accessory. Attach it to a pin or hair comb, or use it to adorn the evening bag you'll make in Lesson 36. (Fig. 6-34)

Foot: Beading for bead application; standard for serge-gathering
Stitch: 3-thread
Stitch length: Standard N—slightly longer than the individual bead
Stitch width: Narrow (use right needle for small pearls, left needle for medium pearls) to cover the bead; widest for serge-gathering
Thread: Matching color
Needle: All-purpose or serger
Upper looper: Monofilament nylon, all-purpose, or serger
Lower looper: All-purpose or serger
Tension: Rolled edge for bead application; balanced for serge-gathering
Needle: Size 11/75
Fabric: 5" of organza or georgette (45" wide)
Notions: 1-1/2 yards of pearl beading

1. Fold the fabric strip in half lengthwise. Serge the pearl beading to the folded edge using the beading foot and a rolled-edge stitch.

2. Change to the standard foot. Adjust your serger for serge-gathering, using one of the techniques in Lesson 23 (page 111). With the presser foot raised, begin the gathering by carefully serging over the pearls at one end. Lower the presser foot and taper to the cut edges, finishing the edges. (Fig. 6-35) Taper off at the other end, raising the presser foot as you serge over the pearls.

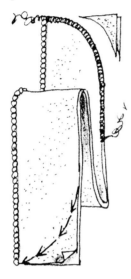

Fig. 6-35: *Taper the strip ends while serge-gathering. Raise the foot when serging over the pearls.*

3. If you want more gathering, pull on the needle thread (the shortest thread in the chain). Shape the strip into a flower and hand-tack the gathered edges together.

Lesson 29. Serge-Couching

Couching braid (for embellishing fabric with curved or looped designs) can be created on your serger. Two options are the puffed serged braid featured in Lesson 20 (page 103)—made by serging over tubes of bias fabric or thick yarn—and the serged couching braid from Lesson 22 (page 109)—serged over water-soluble stabilizer.

Create a simpler couching braid by serging over a filler, such as strands of heavier thread or cord, using a rolled-edge stitch. Use heavier decorative thread in the upper looper and matching all-purpose or serger thread in the needle and lower looper. Place the filler under the back and over the front of the presser foot (or use a beading or ribbon foot), guiding it with the filler-cord techniques from Lesson 4 (page 49).

For a thinner couching braid, use a lighter-weight filler or fewer filler threads. If you use heavy thread in the upper looper, you may choose not to have a filler at all. Adjust your serger for a short, standard N or narrower, and balanced 3-thread stitch. Tighten the lower looper slightly. The lower looper thread should not show, and any filler should be covered entirely by the upper looper thread.

Sew couching braid to your fabric by straight-stitching through it, zigzagging over it, or stitching beside it with a sewing machine blindhem stitch. Straight-stitching works best on thinner, flatter braid. You will often need to blindhem-stitch or zigzag over a thicker braid. (Fig. 6-36) Use monofilament nylon or matching thread in the needle.

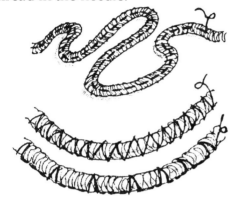

Fig. 6-36: *Straight-stitch flatter couching braid. Zigzag or blindhem-stitch over thicker braid.*

To apply couching directly with your serger, use a balanced or flatlock stitch. This application requires straighter design lines, but loops can be formed in the couching braid to add interest. The loops are later glued, hand-tacked, straight-stitched, or zigzagged down. (Fig. 6-37) Or you may choose to thread a bead on the loop as you work, before securing the second side.

For easier couching application, use a fusible thread in the lower looper when making the simpler couching braid. Loosen the lower looper tension to allow more coverage for the fusible thread. Fuse the braid to your fabric to complete the couching. For more durability after fusing, zigzag over the braid.

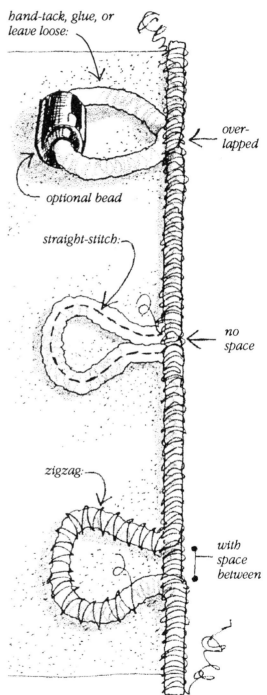

hand-tack, glue, or leave loose:

over-lapped

optional bead

straight-stitch:

no space

zigzag:

with space between

Fig. 6-37: *Serge-couch a straight edge, leaving loops. Variations add interest.*

Project: Couched Tree Ornament

Little couched pillows add a festive touch to any Christmas tree. They're serged quickly with rolled-edge finishing and simple couching braid. Vary the fabric, thread color, and couching design to individualize each ornament. (Fig. 6-38)

Fig. 6-38: *Couching personalizes an easy Christmas ornament.*

Foot: Standard, beading, or ribbon for braid; rolled edge for serge-seaming

Stitch: 3-thread

Stitch length: Short

Stitch width: Standard N or narrower

Thread: Contrasting color
 Needle: Matching
 Upper looper: Woolly nylon
 Lower looper: Fusible for braid; woolly or monofilament nylon for rolled-edge seaming

Tension: Balanced for braid; rolled edge for serge-seaming

Needle: Size 11/75 (14/90 if using fusible thread)

Fabric: 1/6 yard woven fabric

Notions: Heavy filler thread (crochet or pearl cotton); fiberfill for stuffing

1. Cut two 4" fabric squares on the bias grain.

2. With an air-erasable marker, draw a couching design on both squares. Use initials or simple designs such as bells, stars, or Christmas trees. (Use cookie cutters for other shapes.)

3. With a narrow, balanced stitch and your serger threaded according to the specifications above, serge over four strands of filler to create one yard of braid.

4. Fuse the braid over the designs on the squares, tucking the ends underneath. Zigzag over the braid with monofilament nylon thread.

5. Place the two squares wrong sides together, making certain the designs are going in the same direction.

6. Change to the rolled-edge foot and adjust for a rolled-edge stitch. Serge-seam three pillow edges. Stuff the pillow and serge-seam the final edge.

7. Still using the rolled-edge adjustment, serge over two strands of the filler, making a 6" chain. Form the chain into a hanging loop and hand-tack it to the upper corner of the ornament.

7. Decorative Serged Closures

- **Lesson 30. Lapped and Top-stitched Zippers**
- **Lesson 31. Zipped Double-bound Edge**
- **Lesson 32. Serge-picked Zippers**
- **Lesson 33. Serge-bound Buttonholes**
- **Lesson 34. Serged Elastic Button Loops**

Although we have steered away from construction techniques in this book, this chapter is an exception. Decorative closures can be an important design element in your serging projects. For example, a colorful top-stitched zipper down the front of a top or pretty serge-bound buttonholes to match your jacket's edge-finishing provide an outstanding ornamental feature on your garment. In this chapter, we will discuss several favorite decorative closures and the techniques for applying them. None is very complicated, and a few are actually simple.

Lesson 30. Lapped and Top-stitched Zippers

Zippers can be applied to garments and craft projects using several methods. The simplest application involves serge-finishing both fabric edges with a narrow decorative stitch and top-stitching them single-layer to the right side of the zipper tape. This sporty technique leaves the zipper teeth exposed. Colorful zippers and a variety of thread choices lend a wide range of combinations.

Experiment with different edge finishes featured in Chapter 4. Adjust for a short, satin-stitch length for best thread coverage. Test first, though, because too short a stitch can cause an edge to stretch out.

For more durable edges, especially on lightweight or knit fabrics, press under the seam allowance and serge-finish on the fold. Add 1/2" allowances if there are none, press them under, and serge-finish.

Basic lapped and top-stitched zipper

1. With decorative thread in the upper looper, serge-finish the edges to be zipped. Serge from the right side, directly on the seamlines or over the fold.

2. Place the serge-finished edges on the top side of the zipper tape, next to the teeth.

3. Top-stitch with a straight-stitch along the needleline of the serging. (Fig. 7-1)

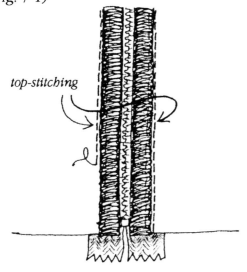

top-stitching

Fig. 7-1: *Top-stitch the lapped zipper next to the needleline of the decorative serging.*

The basic lapped and top-stitched zipper application is most often used when both ends of the zipper will be crossed and anchored by an intersecting seam.

Lapped and top-stitched placket

Create a decorative placket without using a seamline. In this simple technique, the placket is serge-finished in one continuous line. Then it is lapped and top-stitched over the zipper. (Fig. 7-2)

Fig. 7-2: *Easily serge ornamental plackets for neckline and pocket openings.*

1. Draw a line the desired length and location of the zipper opening. Then cut along the line, stopping 1/2" from the end. Make angled cuts at the end of the line, as shown. (Fig. 7-3)

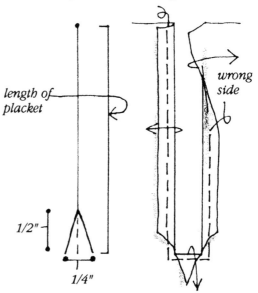

length of placket

wrong side

1/2"

1/4"

Fig. 7-3: *Cut a placket opening, then press the edges to the wrong side and top-stitch.*

2. Fold the cut edges to the wrong side and press. Top-stitch to secure the folds.

3. With a short, narrow, balanced stitch and decorative thread in the upper looper, serge the folded edges. At the bottom of the placket, pull the fabric straight (as you would to serge any inside corner) and serge the entire placket in one continuous line. Any balanced decorative stitch may be used, but a narrow width provides more even stitching at the bottom of the slit.

4. Lap the decoratively serged opening over the zipper and top-stitch close to the serged edge. (Fig. 7-4)

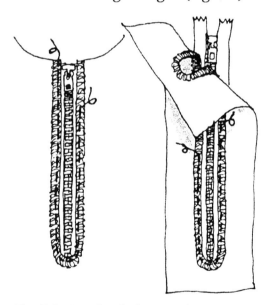

Fig. 7-4: Lap the placket over the zipper and top-stitch close to the serged edge.

Decorative pocket zipper variation: This technique may also be used to apply a zipper to a pocket opening. Cut a slit for the opening

with angled cuts at both ends. Fold and top-stitch the slit as in steps 2 and 3. Remove the thread from the stitch finger and begin serging close to one end of the slit. Serge continuously around the opening, pulling the edges straight at both ends. For a neat finish, overlap the beginning serging using the hidden lapped serging technique on page 34. Tuck the thread tails under when top-stitching the edge to the zipper.

Reversed decorative seam zipper

We introduced a reversed decorative seam on page 35. One of the advantages of this ornamental basic seam is that a section of it can easily be converted to a zipper placket. (Fig. 7-5)

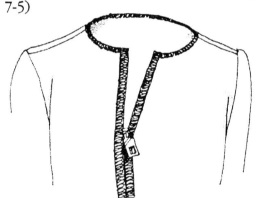

Fig. 7-5: Hide a zipper under a reversed decorative seam.

1. Adjust for the widest, satin-length, and balanced 3-thread stitch using decorative thread in the upper looper, fusible thread in the lower looper, and all-purpose or serger thread in the needle. Tighten the lower looper tension slightly so no fusible thread shows on the top side of the stitching.

2. Serge-finish both edges from the wrong side, positioning the needle on the seamline.

S **Special Tip:** If your fabric has a tendency to stretch, use a positive differential feed (above 1.0), ease-plus manually, or lengthen the stitch slightly. Test first on project scraps.

3. Place the two serge-finished pieces wrong sides together. Using a zipper foot, machine-baste the length of the zipper placket. At the bottom of the placket, adjust to a normal stitch length, back-stitch, and finish seaming. (Fig. 7-6)

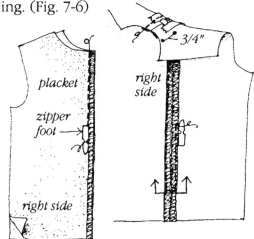

Fig. 7-6: *Machine-baste a zipper placket while straight-stitching a reversed decorative seam. Fuse the allowances before top-stitching them over the zipper.*

4. Using a press cloth, fuse the allowances to the right side of the fabric on both sides of the seamline.

5. Center the basted placket over a face-up zipper with the stops 3/4" from the top edge. Still using the zipper foot, top-stitch the edges of the allowance, catching the zipper tape, as shown. Sew across the bottom of the zipper and up each side. Remove the basting stitches. Sew a hook and thread-chain eye above the zipper when the garment is completed.

Embellished zipper tape

For an even sportier zipped pocket, try featuring a serge-decorated zipper on the outside of the garment. With this method, the zipper should be at least 2" longer than the opening.

1. Adjust for the widest, balanced 3-thread stitch with decorative thread in the upper looper, fusible thread in the lower looper, and all-purpose or serger thread in the needle.

2. Unzip the zipper and serge the right side of the zipper tape, beginning at the upper edge. Serge close to the teeth, trimming the tape as you sew and being careful not to hit the teeth with the needle. Repeat for the other side of the zipper tape, beginning at the lower edge. (Fig. 7-7)

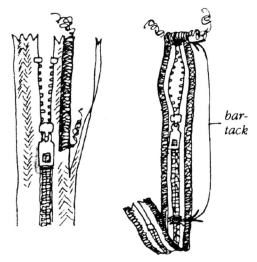

Fig. 7-7: *Decoratively serge-finish the zipper tape on both sides. Bar-tack for the desired finished length and serge-finish the ends.*

3. With the zipper partially open, bar-tack across the teeth at the top of the zipper. Then determine the finished zipper length and bar-tack at the lower edge.

4. Decoratively serge the upper edge of the zipper just above the bartack and the lower edge just below the bartack. Apply seam sealant at the corners and clip the thread chains when dry.

5. Make a slit in the garment or pocket 1/2" less than the length of the finished zipper. With fusible thread in the upper looper and all-purpose or serger thread in the lower looper and needle, serge around the opening

using the techniques for the decorative pocket zipper variation on page 138.

6. Turn back the serged stitching and fuse it to the right side, easing at the corners. (Fig. 7-8)

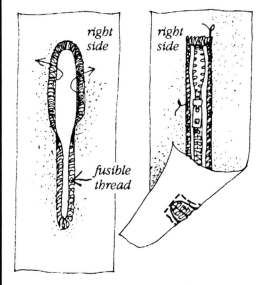

Fig. 7-8: *Fuse the opening edge to the right side, then fuse and top-stitch the zipper over the opening.*

7. Position the zipper over the opening and fuse it in place. For added strength, top-stitch along the outer edges of the decorative serging.

Project: Serged Pencil Case

This zippered pencil case is a quick and easy project for your favorite

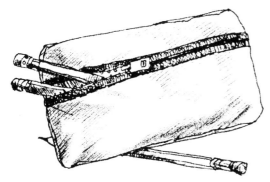

Fig. 7-9: *A sporty pencil case features a colorful lapped and top-stitched zipper.*

student. Select fabrics and decorative edging to suit any taste. (Fig. 7-9)

Foot: Standard
Stitch: 3-thread for decorative; 3- or 3/4-thread for serge-seaming
Stitch length: Short for decorative; standard N for serge-seaming
Stitch width: Standard N for decorative; widest for serge-seaming
Thread: Contrasting color for decorative; matching color for serge-seaming
Needle(s): All-purpose or serger
Upper looper: Cotton crochet for decorative; all-purpose or serger for serge-seaming
Lower looper: All-purpose or serger
Tension: Balanced
Needle(s): Size 14/90
Fabric: 1/6 yard denim (make two cases from 45"-wide fabric)
Notions: One 9" zipper in contrasting color

1. Cut two 10" by 5" rectangles from the denim. Cut one rectangle lengthwise into two pieces, one 10" by 1-1/2" and the other 10" by 3-1/2".

2. Adjust your serger for decorative edging. Serge-finish one long edge of each of the narrower rectangles, trimming slightly.

3. Bar-tack the zipper tape together next to the upper zipper stop with a short zigzag stitch.

4. Center one decorative edge over the right side of the zipper tape. Top-stitch over the needleline of the decorative stitching. Repeat for the other side.

5. Open the zipper and place the two rectangles wrong sides together. The zippered half will be slightly wider than the plain half. Serge-seam all four sides, trimming off the extra fabric. When serging over both ends of the zipper, serge slowly and guide your needle right next to the zipper stops. Turn the case right side out through the zipper opening.

Lesson 31. Zipped Double-bound Edge

This decorative lapped zipper application uses a wide double-bound edge to cover the zipper teeth. Like the basic lapped and top-stitched zipper, the zipped double-bound edge is most often used when both zipper ends will later be intersected by a seam. The zipper pull and teeth will be neatly hidden.

For this application, use the widest stitch on your machine. Cut any edge that will be double-bound 5/8" wider than your pattern. The extra allowance is necessary for the edge-finishing technique.

1. Place the zipper face down on the right side of the seamline, matching the zipper tape to the cut edge.

2. Adjust the serger for a standard N-width, standard N-length stitch. Serge the zipper to the seam allowance, as shown. (Fig. 7-10) Do not trim the

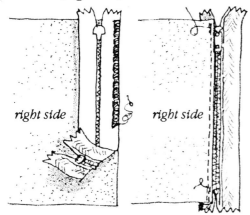

Fig. 7-10: *Serge the zipper to the right side of the fabric. Fold back the allowance and top-stitch.*

zipper tape. Hold the zipper and fabric taut to prevent the presser foot from slipping off the zipper teeth.

3. With the zipper right side up, form a fold in the seam allowance, close to the zipper teeth. Top-stitch the fold to the zipper tape.

4. Finish the fabric for the opposite side of the zipper with a double-bound edge (page 78).

5. Lap the double-bound edge over the zipper teeth and top-stitch in place. If your bound edge is a full 1/2" or more, you may choose to top-stitch on the center needleline. If the binding is narrower, top-stitch over the original top-stitching line.

Project: Dressed-up Cosmetic Bag

A wide double-bound edge hides the zipper on this quilted cosmetic bag. Show off your serging skills and please those on your gift list at the same time. (Fig. 7-11)

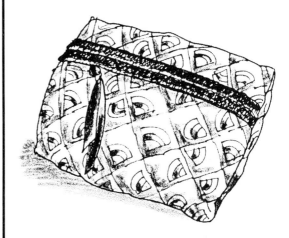

Fig. 7-11: *A double-bound edge hides the zipper on a quilted cosmetic bag.*

Foot: Standard

Stitch: 3-thread for decorative and zipper seaming; 3- or 3/4-thread for serge-seaming

Stitch length: Short for decorative; standard N for serge-seaming

Stitch width: Widest for decorative and serge-seaming; standard N for zipper seaming

Thread: Contrasting color for decorative; matching color for serge-seaming

Needle(s): All-purpose or serger

Upper looper: Two colors of woolly nylon for decorative; all-purpose or serger for serge-seaming

Lower looper: Fusible, all-purpose, or serger for decorative; all-purpose or serger for serge-seaming

Tension: Balanced

Needle(s): Size 11/75

Fabric: 1/3 yard quilted fabric (45"-wide fabric makes five bags)

Notions: One zipper 9" or longer; 6" of 1/4"-wide ribbon

1. Cut an 8" by 12" rectangle from the fabric.

2. Center the right side of the zipper on the right side of one short end of the fabric rectangle, matching the zipper tape to the cut edge. With a standard N stitch width, serge the zipper to the seam allowance.

3. On the other short end, press 3/4" to the wrong side. With decorative thread in the upper looper, serge-finish the fold from the wrong side. Carefully press the serged fold to the right side and top-stitch next to the

overlocked loops. (See instructions for a double-bound edge, page 78.)

4. Fold the remaining fabric edge to the wrong side the same width as your previous decorative stitching. Serge over the fold with a contrasting thread color in the upper looper. Keep the needle right on the needleline of the previous stitching.

5. Lap the decorative edge over the unfinished side of the zipper so that the middle of the binding is next to the zipper teeth. With the zipper closed, top-stitch over the previous needleline, securing the decorative edge to the zipper tape. (Fig. 7-12)

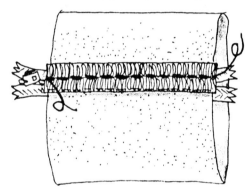

Fig. 7-12: *Top-stitch the decorative binding to the right side of the zipper tape.*

6. Open the zipper and turn the bag inside out. Fold so the zipper is approximately 1-1/2" from the upper edge. Serge-seam the sides of the bag, slowly serging over the zipper tape. (Fig. 7-13)

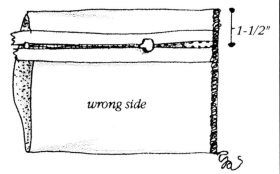

Fig. 7-13: Serge-seam the bag sides from the wrong side.

7. Turn the bag right side out. Knot the ribbon through the zipper pull.

Lesson 32. Serge-picked Zippers

This nifty (yet more complicated) zipper application produces results similar to a hand-picked zipper. Try both the centered and lapped methods in your fashion garments, from tailored to dressy. In addition to the decorative hand-picked look, the zipper is securely sewn to the seam allowance and all edges are neatly serge-finished. (Fig. 7-14)

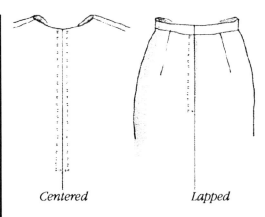

Centered   Lapped

Fig. 7-14: Serge-picked zippers give a decorative, hand-picked appearance.

For a serge-picked zipper, adjust your serger to its longest, widest, balanced 3-thread stitch. Follow the same procedures as when folding for a conventionally sewn blindhem. The needle of the serged stitch should barely catch the fold of the fabric. Stitches will be visible from the right side, but with matching thread they will appear hand-picked.

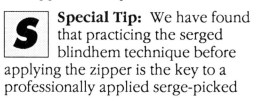 **Special Tip:** We have found that practicing the serged blindhem technique before applying the zipper is the key to a professionally applied serge-picked zipper.

Buy a zipper that is at least 1" longer than the garment opening. The excess zipper will be cut off at the top. For both application methods, machine-baste the opening closed. Press the seam allowances open.

Centered application

1. Place the zipper face down on the basted seam with the teeth directly on the seamline. Machine-baste the zipper to the seam allowance, as shown, ending at the lower zipper stop. (Fig. 7-15)

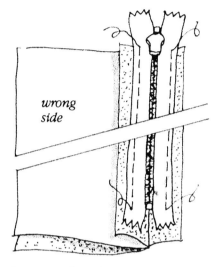

wrong side

Fig. 7-15: Machine-baste the zipper to the seam allowances.

2. Repeat step 1, basting the zipper to the other seam allowance.

3. With the wrong side of the zipper down, fold the fabric exactly 1/4" away from the seamline, as shown. (Fig. 7-16) Serge-pick the zipper, ending even with or above the lower zipper stop, making sure the seam allowance is folded exactly 1/4". Barely catch the needle in the fold of the fabric. The zipper tape and seam allowance will be trimmed slightly. Repeat for the other side of the zipper, starting even with or above the lower stop.

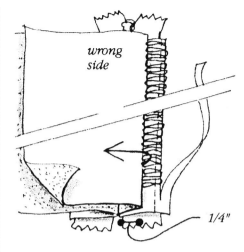

wrong side

1/4"

Fig. 7-16: Fold the fabric back, leaving 1/4" between the seam and foldline. Serge, barely catching the needle in the fold.

4. Pull the garment or project flat and press carefully.

5. To complete the bottom edge of the zipper, fold the fabric back from the lower edge of the zipper. (Fig. 7-17) With chalk or a marking pen,

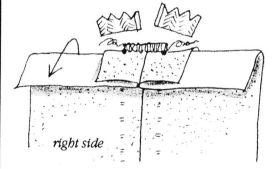

right side

Fig. 7-17: Fold the fabric back at the bottom of the zipper. Trim the zipper tape. Mark and serge-pick the fabric between the needlelines.

mark the needlelines on the fold, as shown. Trim the zipper tape to 1/4". Beginning and ending exactly on the markings, serge-pick the lower edge. Use seam sealant to secure the ends of the serging.

6. Pull the garment flat and press carefully. Remove the machine basting from the seamline.

Lapped application

1. Place the zipper face down on the basted seam with the teeth directly over the seamline.

2. Adjust the serger for a narrow, standard N-length stitch. Serge the zipper to the seam allowance, beginning at the lower zipper stop. (Fig. 7-18) Do not trim the zipper tape.

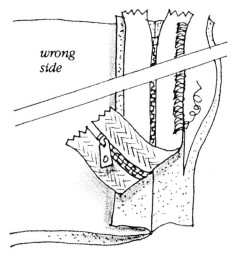

Fig. 7-18: *Center the zipper over the seamline. Beginning at the lower zipper stop, serge the zipper to the right seam allowance.*

Hold the zipper and fabric taut to prevent the presser foot from slipping off the zipper teeth.

3. With the zipper right side up, form a fold in the seam allowance, close to the zipper teeth. Top-stitch the fold to the zipper tape, as shown. (Fig. 7-19)

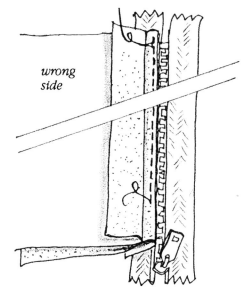

Fig. 7-19: *With the zipper face up, fold the seam allowance close to the teeth. Top-stitch the fold.*

4. With the wrong side of the zipper down, machine-baste the other side of the zipper tape to the seam allowance, beginning even with or above the lower zipper stop.

5. With the wrong side of the zipper still down, fold the fabric exactly 3/8" away from the seamline. (Fig. 7-20) Serge-pick one side as in step 3 of the centered application, beginning even with or above the lower zipper stop.

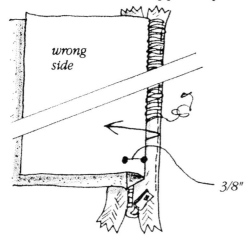

wrong side

3/8"

Fig. 7-20: *Fold the fabric back 3/8". Serge, barely catching the needle in the fold.*

6. Fold the garment back at the bottom of the zipper. Mark, trim, serge-pick, and complete the application as in steps 5 and 6 of the centered method.

Project: Tailored Garment Bag

Although a serge-picked zipper is most often seen in our finest garments, it works equally well for other projects like this sophisticated garment bag. Everyone will think your tailor finished it by hand. (Fig. 7-21)

Fig. 7-21: *Make a tailored garment bag with a centered serge-picked zipper.*

Foot: Standard
Stitch: 3-thread for serge-picking; 3- or 3/4-thread for serge-seaming
Stitch length: Longest for serge-picking; standard N for serge-seaming
Stitch width: Widest
Thread: Matching or contrasting color for serge-picking; matching for serge-seaming
Needle(s): All-purpose or serger
Upper looper: All-purpose or serger
Lower looper: All-purpose or serger
Tension: Balanced
Needle(s): Size 11/75
Fabric: 1-1/2 yards woven fabric— at least 54" wide
Notions: 42" zipper with one zipper pull (purchase from upholstery supply stores or by the yard from mail-order sources)

1. Make the pattern for the back of the garment bag by tracing around a plastic hanger at the top of the bag. Extend the pattern 2" on both sides and 50" in length. Add 1/2" seam allowances to all sides, then curve out the top for the hanger opening. (Fig. 7-22)

2. For the front pattern piece, trace the back and cut it in half lengthwise (for the center front opening). Add 5/8" seam allowances to the center front of both pieces.

3. Cut out the back and the two front pieces.

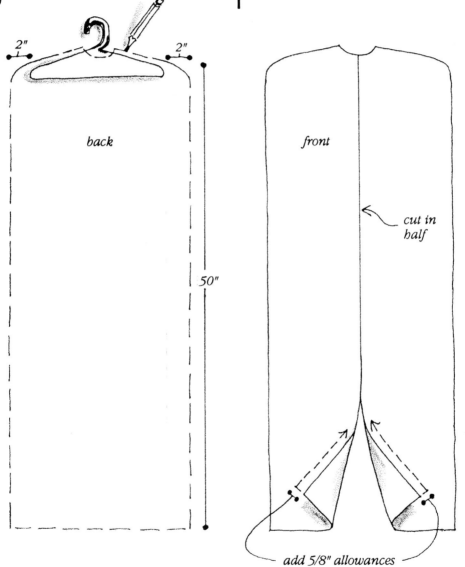

Fig. 7-22: *For the pattern back, trace around the top of a hanger. Add 2" at each side and extend the sides 50". For the front, trace the back and add center seam allowances.*

4. Place the front pieces right sides together. Starting at the top of the bag, straight-stitch the seamline for 2". Back-stitch and lengthen your stitch for machine basting. Continue along the seamline, basting to within 8" of the bottom edge. Switch to a regular straight-stitch. Back-stitch and complete the seam.

5. Place the zipper pull on the upper edge of the zipper and bar-tack 1-1/2" from the top of the zipper tape, making sure the pull is below the bartack.

6. Place the zipper face down on the basted seam, with the teeth directly on the seamline and the top edge of the zipper tape 1/2" from the top edge of the bag. Starting at the top of the zipper tape, machine-baste the center of the zipper tape to the seam allowance on each side, ending 1" from the bottom of the zipper.

7. With the wrong side of the zipper down, fold 1/4" away from the seamline on one side and serge-pick the zipper, barely catching the needle in the fold of the fabric. (Refer back to Fig. 7-16.) Repeat for the other side of the zipper.

8. Pull the bag flat and press carefully. Remove the basting threads.

9. Finish the lower part of the zipper by folding back the bag to the end of the zipper stitching. Trim the zipper to 1/4" and serge-pick between the two needlelines.

10. Serge-finish the top opening edge and the seam allowances below the zipper. Turn the top edge 1/4" to the wrong side and top-stitch to finish.

11. Open the zipper about 12". With right sides together, serge-seam the bottom edge of the bag. Then serge-seam both side seams of the bag. Weave the thread chains back through the serging. Turn the bag right side out through the zipper opening and tie a ribbon or cord to the zipper pull.

Lesson 33. Serge-bound Buttonholes

Buttonholes can be the bane of a sewing project, especially bound buttonholes with their complex and exacting procedure. But with your serger, decorative bound buttonholes are fast and easy. You can also use this technique for decorative welt pockets. Both can complement other decorative serging details on your garment or project.

1. Accurately mark the buttonhole placements on the wrong side of the fabric and on the facing.

2. Using pinking shears, cut rectangles of lightweight nonwoven fusible interfacing for each buttonhole in the fabric and the facing. The rectangles should be 2" wide and 1" longer than the buttonholes. Place the rectangles, resin side up, over the buttonhole positions on the right side of the fabric and facing.

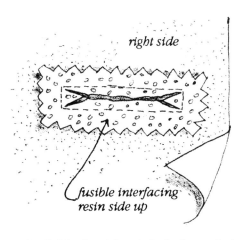

Fig. 7-23: Straight-stitch the buttonhole rectangles from the wrong side, using the markings as a guide.

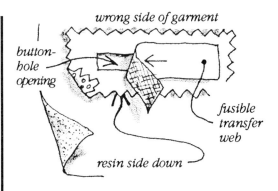

Fig. 7-24: Pull the interfacing to the wrong side of the garment. Finger-press and fuse. Center the transfer web over the opening and press lightly.

3. From the wrong side of the fabric, straight-stitch the buttonhole rectangle markings. (Fig. 7-23)

4. Cut the buttonholes open, clipping to the corners. Carefully turn the interfacing through to the wrong side. Working with the long edges first, finger-press, then fuse, using the tip of your iron.

5. Cut rectangles of paper-backed fusible web 1" wide by 1" longer than the buttonholes. Center them over the wrong side of the buttonhole openings with the web side down. Fuse, remove the paper backings, then trim the web out of the openings. (Fig. 7-24)

6. To make the buttonhole lips, cut a 1"-wide strip of fabric twice the length of each buttonhole plus 2". Fold the strips in half lengthwise with wrong sides together. Serge-finish the folds with a satin length, balanced 3-thread or rolled-edge stitch. This serging is

decorative, so test for the most attractive type and width of stitch for your fabric and pattern. Test different thread types as well.

7. Cut each strip in half and butt the serged edges together. Bar-tack them together at each end to form the buttonhole lips. The bartacks should not show in the finished buttonholes.

8. From the right side, center the buttonhole openings over the right side of the lips and fuse them in place, using a press cloth to prevent shine. (Fig. 7-25)

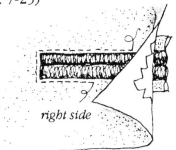

Fig. 7-25: Center the buttonhole over the lips. Fuse them in place and top-stitch.

9. Top-stitch around the boxes, just outside the edges.

10. Fuse the facing to the back side of the buttonholes.

Project: Three-Button Belt

Easy serge-bound buttonholes provide the decorative detail on this *Ultrasuede* belt. It's adjustable by using one, two, or all three button-holes. (Fig. 7-26)

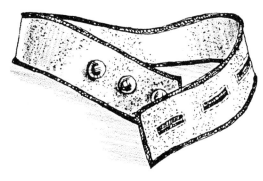

Fig. 7-26: This adjustable belt has three serge-bound buttonholes.

Foot: Standard or rolled edge
Stitch: 3-thread
Stitch length: Short
Stitch width: Narrow or standard N
   with right needle
Thread: Contrasting color
   Needle: All-purpose or serger
   Upper looper: Woolly nylon
   Lower looper: Woolly nylon
Tension: Balanced
Needle: Size 11/75
Fabric: 34" by 4" strip *Ultrasuede*
   for belt (or adjust for your waist
   measurement plus 7"—see note);
   12" by 1" strip lightweight

broadcloth or other woven for buttonhole lips
Notions: 2" by 34" (see note below) stiff fusible interfacing for belt backing; 16" by 2" strip light-weight nonwoven fusible inter-facing for buttonholes; 16" by 1" strip paper-backed fusible web for six buttonhole windows; three 1" buttons

N **Note:** The belt measurements fit a size 27" to 32-1/2" waist. To alter, add to or subtract from the length of both the *Ultrasuede* strip and the stiff fusible interfacing. Use your waist measurement plus 7".

1. Cut the long strip of *Ultrasuede* in half lengthwise. Interface one strip for the top of the belt.

2. Starting 1/2" from one end, mark three 1-1/4" horizontal buttonholes 1-1/2" apart on the wrong side of each strip.

3. Place a 2-1/4" by 2" rectangle of fusible interfacing over the right side of each buttonhole with the resin side up. From the wrong side, straight-stitch buttonhole rectangles over the markings.

4. Cut the buttonholes open, clip-ping to the corners. Turn the interfac-ing to the wrong side, finger-pressing, then fusing.

5. Cut three 2-1/4" by 1" rectangles of transfer web. Center and fuse them over the buttonholes. Remove the paper backings and trim out the openings.

6. Fold the strip of broadcloth in half lengthwise and serge-finish the edge with a narrow satin stitch.

7. Cut six 2" sections from the serged strip. Form three sets of buttonhole lips by butting the serged edges together and bar-tacking very near both ends.

8. Center the wrong side of the belt over the right side of the lips and fuse in place using a press cloth. Top-stitch around the boxes on the outside of the buttonholes. Fuse the wrong side of the under belt to the back of the buttonholes.

9. With wrong sides together, serge around all sides of the belt with a narrow satin stitch to match the buttonhole lips.

10. Attach the buttons to match the buttonholes.

Lesson 34. Serged Elastic Button Loops

For a baby garment or a delicate feminine effect, serge-finish an edge with elastic thread in the lower looper. Then simply pull out elastic button loops at desired intervals for a quick and easy decorative closure.

1. Prepare your serger with decorative thread in the upper looper, elastic thread in the lower looper, and all-purpose or serger thread in the needle.

2. Adjust for a short, standard N or wider stitch. We prefer the 3-thread, although a 3/4-thread stitch looks fine as well. Balance the tension with the upper looper thread slightly wrapping the edge. This makes the elastic invisible from the top side.

 Special Tip: You might have to play with the lower looper (elastic thread) tension to get it adjusted properly because the thread stretches so easily and because elastic thread can vary in weight. Even then, the lower looper thread loops probably will not be precisely even due to the nature of elastic thread. If you cannot loosen the lower looper tension enough, take the elastic thread out of the tension disc (see page 25).

3. After testing the stitch, serge-finish one side of the closure.

4. Use pins to mark equidistant button placements along the outer edge of the serged elastic loops. With a fine crochet hook or tapestry needle, pull the elastic thread at each mark to

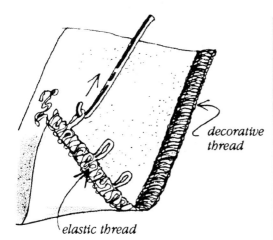

Fig. 7-27: Serge-finish one edge with elastic thread in the lower looper. Pull the elastic to form loops.

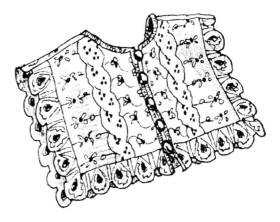

Fig. 7-28: This place-mat collar features a serged elastic button-loop closure.

form small, even loops. (Fig. 7-27) Pulling the elastic thread narrows and tightens the decorative edge slightly and anchors the loops.

5. Change to all-purpose or serger thread in the lower looper and read-just the stitch to match the width and appearance of the decorative serging on the looped edge (now narrower than originally serged because you have pulled the loops).

6. Serge-finish the opposite closure edge. Sew small buttons in the middle of the row of stitching to match the elastic loop placements.

Project: Serge-finished Collar

Select a pretty place mat or dresser scarf for this simple collar. Use serged elastic button loops for the closure. Position the closure on either the front or back of the collar. (Fig. 7-28)

Foot: Standard
Stitch: 3-thread
Stitch length: Short for decorative; standard N for serge-seaming
Stitch width: Widest
Thread: Matching color
    Needle: All-purpose or serger
    Upper looper: Woolly nylon
    Lower looper: Elastic for looped closure; all-purpose or serger for serge-finishing and serge-seaming
Tension: Balanced
Needle: Size 11/75
Fabric: One place mat or dresser scarf with crocheted edging, eyelet, Battenburg lace, or other decorative detailing
Notions: Five or more 7/16" ball buttons

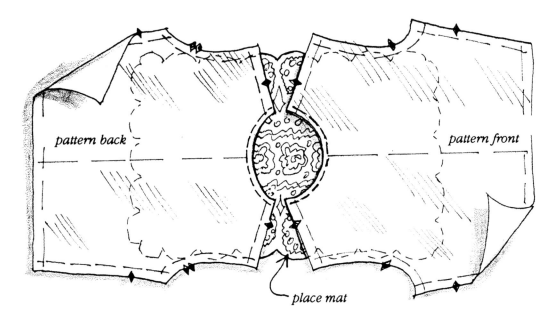

Fig. 7-29: *Cut the collar front and back from a place mat or dresser scarf.*

1. Using a basic jewel-neckline pattern, cut the neckline and shoulder edges for the front and back collar. (Fig. 7-29) Trim 1/2" of the seam allowance from the neckline. Cut along the center front or back for the collar opening.

2. Serge-seam the shoulders with a wide, standard N-length, balanced stitch.

3. Adjust your serger for serged elastic button loops. Serge-finish the right front or the right back.

4. Pull the elastic thread at equidistant intervals to form button loops. The number of loops and their spacing depend on the depth of your collar and the desired effect.

5. Rethread the lower looper and readjust for matching decorative stitching. Serge-finish the other side of the opening.

6. Fold 1/8" of the neckline to the wrong side and serge-finish with the same stitch adjustment as in step 5. Thread the chain tails back through the stitches to secure.

7. Attach buttons to match the loop placements.

8. Expanding Your Artistic Possibilities

- **Lesson 35. Serger Chain Art**
- **Lesson 36. Serged Appliqué**
- **Lesson 37. Serger Cutwork**
- **Lesson 38. Embellished Fabric**

In previous chapters we discussed traditional decorative seaming, edge-finishing, and special techniques. We also included a number of brand-new serger applications that we discovered during our research for this book series. Serge-bound seams and edges, clear elastic trim and piping, picot braid, and serged elastic button loops are some notable examples.

For this final chapter, we will cover creative possibilities that usually aren't associated with serger sewing. Although we had done some work with serger chain, appliqué, cutwork, and fabric embellishment in the past (see our two books, *Distinctive Serger Gifts & Crafts* and *Simply Serge Any Fabric*), we felt that we had barely begun to explore these areas.

Having the time to test and develop more ideas was the major factor limiting our research. Yet artistic possibilities seem endless, including combinations of decorative techniques and unusual applications for existing techniques, as well as the continual introduction of new products and technology. What we have included in these last four lessons is merely a starting point—for us and, we hope, for you—to push the serger to its creative limits.

Lesson 35. Serger Chain Art

Originally used for professional-looking button and belt loops, serger chain has now become an exciting medium for artistic expression in both craft and dressmaking projects. With the wide array of decorative threads and yarns available for serger use, possibilities abound for interesting chain projects. And the speedy serger can make yards and yards of serger chain in minimal time.

Now we've begun to explore serger-chain tassels, fringe, cording, and jewelry. (Fig. 8-1) Although

Fig. 8-1: Artistic uses for serger chain include tassels, fringe, cording, and jewelry.

some of these projects are more craft-oriented, others can be used to ornament your latest fashion garments. And you won't have to worry about not finding the perfect color or texture—you can coordinate it yourself.

1. To make a conventional serger thread chain, remove the presser foot and adjust your machine for a rolled-edge stitch.

2. Put the thread, yarn, or ribbon you want to feature in the upper looper. This thread will be the most visible in the chain. Anything you can serge with is possible. Try ribbon floss, fine yarn, or any decorative thread.

3. Thread the needle with a light-weight matching or monofilament nylon thread. This thread will be the least visible in the chain. For variety, test other lightweight threads. Fine

metallic thread adds a touch of sparkle, while top-stitching thread changes the texture or color.

4. Use woolly or monofilament nylon in the lower looper for the tightest rolled-edge stitch and the firmest chain. Tighten the lower looper tension as much as possible when using shiny thread such as rayon in the upper looper.

 Special Tip: You may find it impossible to form a tightly rolled edge with a slippery thread in the upper looper. If so, try instead to make a flatter chain by tightening the upper looper tension, too, for a more balanced stitch.

5. Adjust your stitch length and tensions for the thread you're using. When using heavy thread such as pearl cotton or crochet thread, start with a standard N stitch length and shorten it gradually to get the most attractive stitch formation. If the stitch length is too short, the thread can jam at the presser foot.

6. Hold the thread chain taut for a more uniform chain. If there are skipped stitches in the chain, try switching to a size 14/90 needle. Also try loosening the tensions a small amount, one at a time. First adjust the lower looper, then the upper looper, and finally the needle.

Test unusual serger-chain stitching options. Vary the stitch size and tensions. Try serging over one or more strands of heavy filler thread. Or, for more options, substitute fine wire for the filler thread. (We'll use fine wire later in this lesson to wrap a tassel.) Puffed serged braid (page 103) is actually a serger-chain variation made with balanced tension and a thicker filler.

Thread-chain cording

Make cording from serger thread chain by using the bobbin winder on your sewing machine.

1. Knot one or more long strands of serger chain through a hole in the bobbin. (Fig. 8-2) The strand(s)

Fig. 8-2: Attach serged chain strands to the bobbin and wind. Hold the cording at the halfway point and wind the outer half back onto the bobbin half.

should be twice as long as the desired cording length. The length of the strand is limited by the length of your arms, unless you have one person run the machine while another holds the chain.

2. Hold the free end of the serger chain securely. Wind the bobbin until the strands are firmly twisted.

3. Before removing the cording from the bobbin, hold the twisted strands at the halfway point with your other hand. The cording will automatically twist back on itself. Pull the cording until the twisting is uniform.

Thread-chain cording may be used for decorative accents (such as edge trimming or couching), accessory items (necklaces or belts), or home decoration (pillow trims and drapery tie-backs).

 Special Tip: For heavy cording that is too thick to tie to a bobbin, have one person hold one end of the strand(s) while another person does the twisting. Or tie one end to a doorknob on a closed door and twist from the free end.

Thread-chain fringe

Make your own matching or decorative fringe from serger thread chain. For 1" fringe, cut a piece of tear-away stabilizer 3" wide by the desired length. Fold it lengthwise into a 1" width (3 layers). Vary the width of the stabilizer to change the length of the fringe. Loosely wrap the serger chain around the stabilizer. With a wide, satin-length, balanced stitch, serge along one edge with the same decorative thread in the upper looper. (Fig. 8-3) Dab seam sealant on the chains

tear-away stabilizer layers

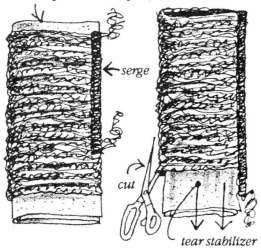

Fig. 8-3: *Wrap the chain around the stabilizer. Serge the upper edge and cut the lower edge. Tear away the stabilizer for the finished fringe.*

on the other edge so they won't ravel. Allow them to dry, then cut. Tear away the stabilizer. Top-stitch the fringe to your project through the upper row of stitching.

Thread-chain tassels

Make tassels from any size of serger thread chain. (Fig. 8-4) For a delicate tassel, use rayon, lingerie, or fine metallic thread. Try pearl cotton, pearl rayon, or crochet thread for a heavier tassel. Rayon thread will make the smoothest chain. Serge at least six yards of chain for one tassel. Smaller chain will require more strands for a fuller appearance.

Fig. 8-4: *Make tassels from any size serger chain.*

1. Loosely wind the chain over a firm piece of cardboard cut to the length of your tassel. The more chain that is wrapped, the fuller the tassel. Do not stretch the chain while winding.

2. Cut a 6" strand of chain for the tassel hanger. Tie the chain together at one end of the cardboard, as shown. (Fig. 8-5) Dab seam sealant

Fig. 8-5: *Tie the chain together at one end of the cardboard.*

on the chains on the opposite end of the cardboard so they won't ravel. Allow them to dry before cutting.

3. About 3/4" below the tied end, form a loop of chain and wrap over it. After you have completed the wrapping, thread the chain ends through the loop and pull to secure. (Fig. 8-6) Hide the ends under the edge of the wrapping.

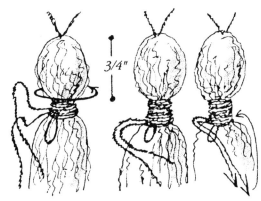

Fig. 8-6: *Form a thread-chain loop and wrap over it. Pull the ends through the loop to secure. Tuck the tails under the wrapping.*

 Optional: Serge an 8" chain strand over fine wire using the techniques in Lesson 7 (page 63). Wrap the tassel, twist the ends together, and tuck them under the wrapping.

Project: Double-wrapped Tassel

Make two tassels to finish the ends of the table runner in Lesson 15 (page 86). (Fig. 8-7) Test matching metallic

Fig. 8-7: *These simple thread-chain tassels feature two wrappings. Attach them to the table runner from Lesson 15.*

yarn in a chain before using it for the tassels. If you find that it is too wiry, choose a matching color of softer heavy rayon thread.

Foot: Removed
Stitch: 3-thread
Stitch length: Short
Stitch width: Any
Thread: Matching color
    Needle: All-purpose or serger
    Upper looper: Decorative thread
    Lower looper: Woolly nylon
Tension: Rolled edge
Needle: Size 11/75
Notions: 16" of 24-gauge fine, flexible wire (such as bead wire, purchased at a craft store); a small amount of yarn in a matching color (enough to form two 3/4" balls); cardboard

1. Serge 22 yards of chain for two tassels. With the same serger adjustments and decorative thread, carefully serge over the wire.

2. Cut off 48" of chain and section it into four 12" pieces.

3. For each tassel, loosely wrap half the long chain around a 5" piece of cardboard. Tie the chains together at one end of the cardboard using one of the shorter chains. (See Fig. 8-5.)

4. Dab seam sealant on the thread chains at the opposite end so they won't ravel. Allow them to dry, then cut the ends evenly.

5. With the other 12" chains, wrap each tassel together tightly about 3/4" from the top. Secure the ends by placing them through the loop, as shown in step 3 of the previous thread-chain tassel instructions.

6. Wind the matching yarn into balls and insert them between the thread-chain strands close to the wrapped sections.

7. With 8" of the wire, wrap each tassel tightly, enclosing and securing the yarn ball. Insert the wire ends under the wrapped edges. Adjust the thread chains to cover the yarn. (Fig. 8-8) (Or use two additional 12" chains to wrap the tassels as in step 5 above.)

Twist wire ends together and tuck under

Fig. 8-8: *Use chain serged over fine wire to wrap tassels.*

8. Hand-tack the tassels to each end of the table runner, covering the serging joints.

Lesson 36.
Serged Appliqué

Appliqué is one of our favorite embellishments because it offers so many options for creativity. You can use it to add texture, color, and a three-dimensional effect to any fabric. Fashion your own design to adorn your latest garments, sweaters, accessories, or home decoration projects.

In the past, we've worked with flat and 3-D appliqué. We've also tried padded appliqué. Just about any serged edge-finish or trim can be used. Other techniques such as serger lace and serging over sequins, beads, or pearls adapt well to appliqué. Let your creativity guide you.

Serge-finish the edges of the pieces you plan to appliqué. A satin rolled-edge stitch is the most common for edge finishing, but any serged edge is possible.

Apply the appliqué pieces to your fabric by top-stitching all of the edges flat, top-stitching only part of the edges (for a raised or 3-D appliqué), or attaching them by hand-tacking, fusing, or fabric painting. (Fig. 8-9)

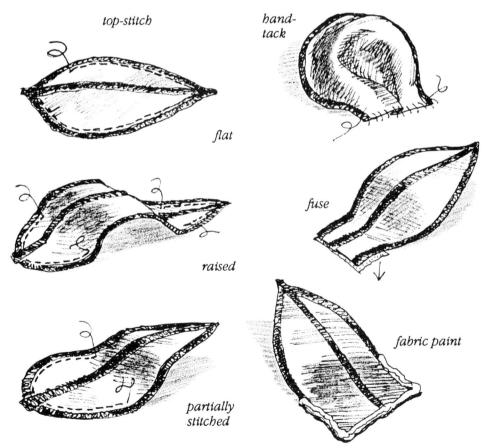

top-stitch

flat

hand-tack

raised

fuse

partially stitched

fabric paint

Fig. 8-9: *Appliqué serge-finished pieces to your project fabric.*

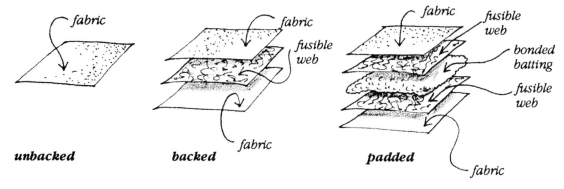

fabric

fabric

fusible web

fabric

fusible web

bonded batting

fusible web

fabric

unbacked   **backed**   **padded**

fabric

Fig. 8-10: *Appliqués can be cut from backed, unbacked, or padded fabric.*

Appliqués may be unbacked, backed, or padded. (Fig. 8-10) Unbacked appliqués are usually applied flat to the project fabric with the under side of the appliqué fabric hidden. Make backed appliqués simply by sandwiching a layer of fusible transfer web between two layers of fabric (right sides out) so that both sides of the appliqué will appear finished when they are applied by the raised or 3-D methods.

Make padded appliqués by sandwiching bonded batting between two layers of fusible transfer web. Then fuse the batting and web between two layers of fabric, with the web against the wrong side of the fabric. Padded appliqués are most often applied raised or 3-D, in the same manner as unpadded, backed appliqués.

Project: Appliquéd Evening Bag

Serged appliqué adorns this unique evening bag. Make the strap by cording thread chain, then top the bag with the pearl-trimmed organdy flower made in Lesson 28 (page 132). (Fig. 8-11)

Fig. 8-11: *Construct an appliquéd evening bag with a cording strap, satin leaves, and the flower from Lesson 28.*

Foot: Rolled edge for appliqué;
   standard for serge-seaming
Stitch: 3-thread for appliqué; 3- or
   3/4-thread for serge-seaming
Stitch length: Short for appliqué;
   standard N for serge-seaming
Stitch width: Standard N for
   appliqué; widest for serge-seam-
   ing
Thread: Matching color
   Needle(s): All-purpose or serger
   Upper looper: Rayon or other
      decorative for appliqué; all-
      purpose or serger for serge-
      seaming
   Lower looper: Woolly nylon for
      appliqué; all-purpose or serger
      for serge-seaming
Tension: Rolled edge for appliqué;
   balanced for serge-seaming
Needle(s): Size 11/75
Fabric: 1/2 yard taffeta for outer
   bag; 1/2 yard matching lining
   fabric for bag lining; 1/6 yard
   matching satin for appliquéd
   leaves
Notions: 10" polyester fleece; 10"
   heavy fusible interfacing; 6" by
   12" piece paper-backed fusible
   web; one spool matching ribbon
   floss for strap; one large snap

1. Cut 10" by 18" rectangles from the
taffeta, lining, fleece, and interfacing.
Fuse the interfacing to the fleece.

2. From the ribbon floss, make one
yard of thread-chain cording, following the instructions on page 157.

3. Match the ends of the cording to
the cut edges of the right side of the
lining 6-1/2" from the top on both
sides. (Fig. 8-12) With the right sides

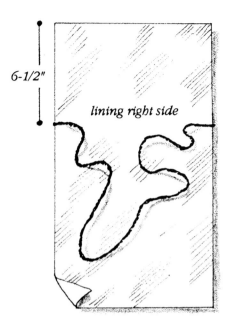

Fig. 8-12: *Position the cording on top of the lining.*

of the taffeta and lining together,
place the fleece on top of the taffeta.

4. Serge-seam the four sides of the
bag, leaving an opening at the lower
edge for turning and being careful not
to catch the cording in the serging.
Secure the cording in the seam by
straight-stitching again over the cording with a short stitch length.

5. Turn the bag to the right side and
fold the opening allowances to the
inside. Press carefully. Edge-stitch
across the lower edge, closing the
opening.

6. At the lower edge, fold 4-1/2" to
the wrong side to form the bag. From

the right side of the bag, edge-stitch the three unfolded edges. (Fig. 8-13)

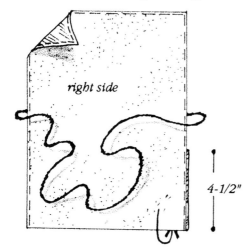

right side

4-1/2"

Fig. 8-13: *Fold up the lower edge to form a pocket. Edge-stitch.*

7. Fold the upper edge down even with the cording placement, forming the flap. Press lightly.

8. To make the leaf appliqué, fuse the transfer web to the back of the satin fabric. Remove the paper backing and fuse the other side to the wrong side of a matching rectangle of the satin. Using the grid as a pattern, cut one large leaf and one small leaf set from the fused satin. (Fig. 8-14)

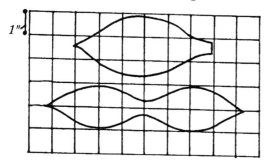

1"

Fig. 8-14: *Pattern for the large leaf and small leaf set.*

9. With your serger adjusted for appliqué sewing (see the specifications on page 163), fold the leaves in half lengthwise and serge the folded edge, forming the leaf ribs. (Fig. 8-15) Pull the leaves flat and serge-finish all leaf edges.

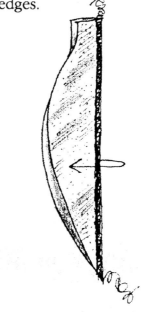

Fig. 8-15: *Fold the leaf in half and serge the fold with a satin rolled edge.*

10. Place the large leaf on the bag flap, raising the center rib three-dimensionally. Top-stitch both sides, starting and ending about 1-1/2" from the leaf ends.

11. Pin a tuck in the middle of the smaller leaf set and place it over the larger leaf, as shown. (Fig. 8-16) Top-stitch both leaves as you did the larger one. Straight-stitch across the bottom of all three leaves to secure.

Fig. 8-16: Appliqué the leaves to the bag flap.

12. Attach the flower made in Lesson 28 over the center of the leaves. Hand-sew the large snap, securing the flap to the top of the bag.

Lesson 37.
Serger Cutwork

Our first introduction to serger cutwork was when Sue Green-Baker wrote about it for our *Serger Update* newsletter in early 1988. Although it was a fascinating technique, it took considerable skill and patience to serge-finish the inner edge of small holes cut in a piece of fabric. (Fig. 8-17)

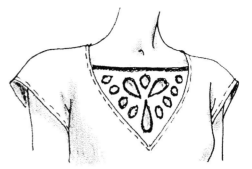

difficult serge-finishing method

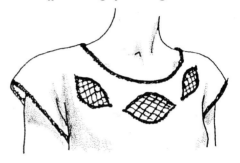

easy water-soluble stabilizer method

Fig. 8-17: Serger cutwork options.

Then we discovered an interesting new product—water-soluble stabilizer—and Naomi started experimenting. The results were a speedy combination of sewing and serging that created an interesting new appliquéd cutwork.

This newer method works equally well for garments, table linens, and craft projects. The cutwork appliqué must be applied to a washable fabric because the washable stabilizer has to be dissolved in water to complete the project.

Serging over the stabilizer gives stitches a stiff, starched effect. Test various threads and stitch types for the desired effect. For example, woolly nylon in a satin rolled edge creates a stiff design. With a longer, balanced stitch, it gives a softer appearance.

1. With a water-soluble pen, draw a cutwork design outline on the project fabric. (Fig. 8-18)

2. Cut a piece of water-soluble stabilizer larger than the design on all sides. Allow an extra 1/4" for each line of serging you will be applying, then add an additional inch on each side of the piece.

3. Draw serging guidelines onto the stabilizer. (Fig. 8-18) For more dura-

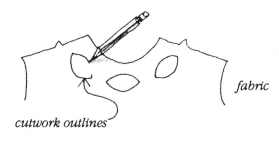

cutwork outlines

fabric

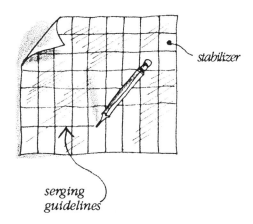

stabilizer

serging guidelines

Fig. 8-18: *Draw cutwork outlines on the fabric and serging guidelines on the water-soluble stabilizer.*

bility, draw the guidelines close together and limit the size of the appliqué. Plan straight rows of serging for your first project because serging a curved fold can by tricky.

 Optional: For a quick project, don't bother to draw guidelines. Just serge parallel rows a presser-foot width apart, using the foot as a guide.

4. Fold the stabilizer on the guidelines and serge over the folds with a stitch adjustment you have previously tested. (Don't worry if you cut the stabilizer.)

5. Place the decorated stabilizer over the design outline on the right side of the base fabric. Use an embroidery hoop to align the two layers and hold them flat. (Fig. 8-19) Be sure the

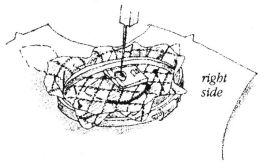

right side

Fig. 8-19: *Align the serged stabilizer over the cutwork outline using an embroidery hoop. Zigzag the stitched stabilizer to the fabric.*

serged stitches extend past the design outline on all sides.

6. With matching thread and a narrow, satin stitch, zigzag the stabilizer to the fabric following the design outline.

7. Remove the hoop and carefully trim the stabilizer close to the outside of the zigzag stitch. Then trim away the fabric from behind the stabilizer appliqué. Be careful not to cut the zigzag stitch or the fabric. (Fig. 8-20)

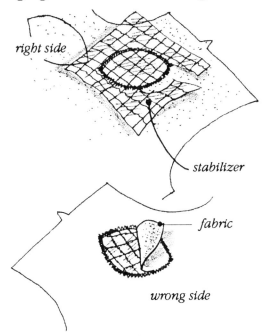

Fig. 8-20: Trim the stabilizer outside the zigzagging on the front. Trim the fabric inside the zigzagging on the back.

8. Place another piece of water-soluble stabilizer over the right side of the appliqué and secure both layers in the embroidery hoop. To finish and secure the cutwork, stitch through the stabilizer over the original zigzagging. Use a narrow, satin-length zigzag stitch just a little wider than the original stitching in step 6.

9. Trim away the stabilizer from both sides of the stitching, then submerge

the cutwork appliqué in water to remove the excess. Allow the project to air-dry, or press it dry between two press cloths.

Project: Cutwork Tablecloth

Feature a cutwork motif on one or more corners of a square card-table cloth. Or change measurements for an elegant dresser scarf. (Fig. 8-21)

Fig. 8-21: Embellish a tablecloth with appliquéd cutwork.

Foot: Rolled edge
Stitch: Rolled edge
Stitch length: Short
Stitch width: Standard N
Thread: Matching color
    Needle: All-purpose or serger
    Upper looper: All-purpose or serger
    Lower looper: All-purpose or serger
Tension: Rolled edge

Needle: Size 11/75
Fabric: 54" by 54" square lightweight linen-like fabric
Optional: Use a 14" by 54" rectangle of the same fabric for a
dresser scarf.
Notions: Two 6" by 6" squares
water-soluble stabilizer; air-
erasable or water-soluble marker

1. Serge-finish all four edges of the
fabric with a narrow rolled edge,
serging on and off at each corner.
Secure the thread chains with seam
sealant and clip the tails when dry.

 Optional: With a 3/4-thread
machine, you may choose to
use the tuck-and-roll (see
page 59) instead of a plain rolled edge
for a more elaborate finish.

2. Draw a 4" oval in the corner of the
tablecloth using the marker.

3. Serge the stabilizer with rows of
stitching in a crisscrossed design of
your choice. Extend the rows of
serging to fill the stabilizer square.

4. Center the serged stabilizer over
the oval and apply it to the tablecloth
following the previous instructions for
serged cutwork.

Lesson 38.
Embellished Fabric

Although there is a difference
between actually constructing yardage
on your serger and ornamenting fabric
by adding serged stitches and detail,
we group them together here.

Constructing fabric

Using a serger to construct patchwork fabric has been explored in
detail by many sewing professionals.
Myriad patchwork designs are possible, and they can be constructed
more quickly than with a sewing
machine because of the serger's faster
stitching.

Another option for constructing
decorative fabric on your serger is to
mix fabric types, textures, or colors to
complement the design of your garment. The method of seaming the
elements together can be decorative
as well. Exposed seams of any type or
color are an option.

Inserts are yet another way to create
unusual fabric for your project. Strips
of synthetic suede or leather can be
placed strategically in the middle of
your fashion fabric. Tapestry insets
add a hand-detailed effect. Or a
lighter-weight fabric strip can be
serge-gathered on both long edges
and inserted as a decorative detail.
(Fig. 8-22)

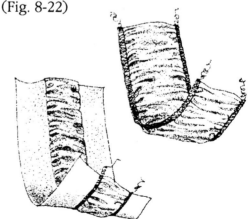

Fig. 8-22: *Serge-gather a fabric strip and
inset into yardage.*

Ornamenting fabric

Heirloom serging (a replication of French hand-sewing) was an early example of serger-embellished fabric. Delicate rows of pintucks, lace inserts, and rolled edges can be applied quickly to a fabric such as batiste, organdy, or handkerchief linen. An art in itself, beautiful heirloom serging has been featured extensively in books and articles.

We want to take the art of ornamenting fabric one step further. You don't have to use dainty stitches on lightweight woven fabrics in straight rows to embellish your fabric. Consider all of your ornamental serging possibilities. Most edge-finishes also can be serged over folds, so you have the option of placing stitches anywhere on your fabric—and in any direction.

Try diagonal or vertical rows of corded rolled edges, perhaps to accent a stripe in the fabric. Test parallel rows of wide, balanced, satin serging to duplicate current designer fabrics. (Or try prepleating a fabric with a *Perfect Pleater* device and serge-finishing each tuck.) Consider serging with uneven spacing, sporadically placed stitching, or combinations of techniques. (Fig. 8-23)

The 2-thread double chainstitch available on the 797 model (see page 10) can also be used to serge a design or at random on the fabric. Remove the presser foot and hold the fabric taut while serging.

Experiment with all fabric types and any decorative thread. Test ideas from ready-to-wear. Let your imagination soar. We include a few test results here, but these are only the beginning. There's plenty of room for innovation in serger sewing. Have fun, experiment, and let us know what you discover.

Chain-loop serging—Our first idea for this technique was to serge on and off a fold or edge, using a satin rolled edge and leaving thread-chain loops at intervals along the stitching. We serged for a distance and then chained

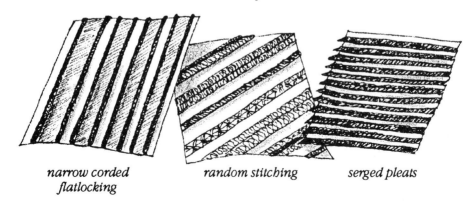

narrow corded
flatlocking   random stitching   serged pleats

Fig. 8-23: *Ornament fabrics with corded flatlocking on stripes, random diagonal stitches, or narrow serged pleats.*

off the fabric. To form a loop, we raised the presser foot, anchored the needle right where the chain left the fabric, and began serging again.

Although we achieved an interesting effect, the method was slow and tedious. Naomi discovered a faster, more random effect by raising the front of the presser foot only to insert the fabric. She was also successful in serging with the presser foot removed the entire time. She was able to chain off and on easily (see Fig. 8-26). Leave the chain in loops or cut it at varying lengths. Don't worry if you cut the fabric while serging; the rolled edge covers any cuts. We've used this technique for the scarf project that follows.

Flatlocked patches—With a heavier thread such as pearl rayon in the upper looper, create short patches of flatlocking in the middle of your fabric, leaving thread tails at each end. Tie beads onto the tails for an added ornamental touch. (Fig. 8-24) Mark

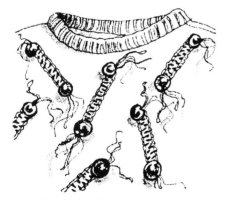

Fig. 8-24: *Flatlock random patches on your fabric. Tie beads onto the tails.*

the placement of your flatlocked patches or apply them randomly. Fold along the placement line. Remove the stitches from the stitch finger and pull out about 3" of unchained thread. Raise the presser foot and anchor the needle at the end of the placement line.

Flatlock the patch, lift the presser foot, remove the stitches from the stitch finger, and pull the threads away from the serging. Do not chain off. Knot the threads at each end or attach beads to secure the stitching. Or if you prefer, pull the thread ends through to the wrong side of the fabric for securing.

Try decorative patches using a rolled-edge or narrow, balanced stitch. Or try chaining on and off the fabric for a different effect.

Finger tensioning—We used finger tensioning on the needle thread to gather lightweight fabric in Lesson 23 (page 112). It also can be used to vary the look of your decorative stitching.

Try applying tension on the looper threads as well. We found that we could create a variety of interesting effects. With a satin-length, standard N-width, balanced stitch and the rolled-edge foot, we used **lower looper tensioning** to create a delicately scalloped edge. (Fig. 8-25)

Using **upper looper tensioning,** we created an unusual scalloped pattern on the top side of a balanced satin stitch. The pattern worked best for us using a satin-length, 4mm-width, balanced stitch and the stan-

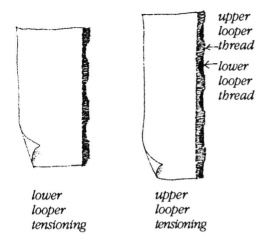

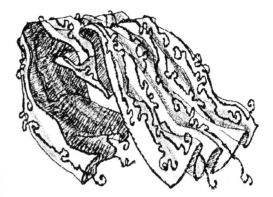

Fig. 8-26: Add free-form embellishment to a long chiffon scarf.

Fig. 8-25: Use lower looper tensioning to create a scalloped rolled edge. Or try upper looper tensioning for a scalloped pattern on top of the stitching.

dard presser foot. With contrasting thread colors in the loopers, we applied upper-looper finger tensioning at regular intervals to form the pattern.

Don't be afraid to experiment with finger tensioning on all of your threads. Results can vary from machine to machine. Try using both a rolled edge and a balanced stitch. Test with different threads, stitch widths, and lengths.

Project: Embellished Chiffon Scarf

Embellish a fashionable two-yard chiffon scarf with random decorative serging for an attention-getting accessory. (Fig. 8-26)

Foot: Rolled edge
Stitch: 3-thread
Stitch length: Short
Stitch width: Standard N
Thread: Contrasting color
    Needle: All-purpose or serger
    Upper looper: Woolly nylon
    Lower looper: Woolly nylon
Tension: Rolled edge
Needle: Size 11/75
Fabric: 2 yards chiffon
Notions: **Optional**—ornamental
    beads to tie on thread-chain tails

1. Cut a piece of chiffon the length of the fabric by 18" wide. Finish all four sides with a rolled edge.

2. Using the techniques described above under chain-loop serging, fill the scarf with random rows of decorative serging. The serging need not be done on the straight of grain. Let a random pattern add to the decorative effect.

3. Leave the chain loops or clip them apart at varying lengths. Tie on ornamental beads if desired.

Pfaff Hobbylock *History*

German musical-instrument maker Georg Michael Pfaff visited London's World Fair in 1850, witnessed the introduction of a machine that was able to sew, and became fascinated with the concept. He later built his first sewing machine and founded a company which was to become one of the world's foremost sewing-machine manufacturers.

The Pfaff family capably steered the company into the second half of the twentieth century when it became publicly owned. Pfaff had already built one million sewing machines by 1910. Destroyed during World War II and later rebuilt, the company celebrated its 125th anniversary in 1987.

This German-based company is well known world wide for quality engineering and reliable machines.

They currently sell both industrial and home-sewing models in 130 different countries and are the largest sewing machine manufacturer in Europe.

Recent Pfaff developments include a computerized sewing machine with a scanner for customized embroidery, a memory that can hold over 3,200 stitches, and many other unique features. Their sergers also feature Pfaff electronics and engineering.

Pfaff American Sales Corp. is the American branch of the company. They first introduced the serger to the home-sewing market in 1985. It's rapid popularity has already led to the next generation of sergers—current models are now designed to easily perform all of the techniques of ornamental serging.

Glossary of Serging Terms

All-purpose or serger thread—All-purpose thread usually means cotton-covered polyester wound parallel on conventional spools. Standard serger thread has the same fiber content but is lighter in weight than all-purpose thread and is cross-wound on cones or tubes so that it can feed more easily during higher-speed serger sewing.

Balanced stitch—A serge-finished edge or seam in which the upper- and lower-looper thread tensions are balanced so the threads meet at the edge of the fabric, forming loops.

Binding—A strip of fabric sewn to an edge, then wrapped around it and secured to hide the seam and the raw edge.

Bite—The distance between the knife and the needle, affecting the amount of fabric in the stitch.

Decorative seam (also decorative exposed seam)—Any seam on the outside of a garment or project that enhances design detail.

Decorative thread (also decorative serging or decorative finish)—Any thread other than all-purpose or serger thread, although even a contrasting color of these threads is technically considered decorative. Our favorite decorative threads include woolly nylon, rayon, pearl cotton, silk, buttonhole twist, and metallic. New threads are introduced regularly.

Ease plus—A manual option to the differential feed, accomplished by force-feeding fabric under the front of the presser foot and holding it from exiting out the back.

Edge-stitch—A medium-length (10-12 stitches/inch), straight-stitch on a conventional sewing machine applied near the edge of anything being sewn. Edge-stitching is often used to join two serge-finished layers.

Filler-cord—Crochet thread, pearl cotton, or buttonhole twist that simulates piping when serged over with a short, satin-length stitch.

Flatlock—A technique by which the needle thread is loose enough so the serged stitches flatten out on top of the fabric, forming decorative loops when the fabric is pulled apart. The underside will show a ladder effect of evenly spaced double parallel stitches. Used for both seaming and decorative stitching on a folded edge, flatlocking

lends many creative possibilities. A 3-thread (and even 3/4-thread) stitch can be adjusted to flatlock.

Heavy thread—Crochet thread, pearl cotton, or buttonhole twist used for serge-gathering or filler-cord in serger piping.

Long stitch—A 4mm or 5mm serged stitch length.

Machine baste—A long (6-8 stitches/inch) straight-stitch on a conventional sewing machine.

Mail order—A growing trend that offers the convenience of at-home catalog shopping. Almost any product is available through mail order, but without the immediate, hands-on selection available at your local fabric store.

Matching thread—Thread the same color as (or that blends as well as possible with) the project fabric.

Medium-length stitch—A serged stitch length of about 3mm, the standard N setting on the *Hobbylock*.

Medium-width stitch—A serged stitch width of about 3.5mm, the standard N setting on the *Hobbylock*.

Mez Alcazar—A quality, 100% rayon, embroidery-weight thread sold only by authorized Pfaff dealers.

Narrow-width stitch—A 2mm or 3mm serged stitch width. Used to serge a narrow seam or edge.

Ornamental serging (also decorative serging)—Any serger stitching used to artistically enhance a garment or project. Decorative thread, altered tension, or a combination of serging techniques can be used to create ornamental serging.

Ready-to-wear—Garments available for purchase through retail stores and mail-order outlets.

Rolled edge (finish or seam)—Also called a narrow rolled edge or hem, this stitch is created by altering the tension so that the raw edge rolls to the underside. A short stitch length creates an attractive satin-stitch edge.

Satin stitch (satin length)—A stitch length short enough to allow the thread used to cover the entire fabric over which it is serged. Appropriate for both a balanced stitch or a rolled edge. To prevent jamming when using this stitch, start with a standard N stitch length and shorten the stitch as needed for the most attractive satin finish.

Serge-finish—Most often a standard N-length, standard N-width, and balanced 3- or 3/4-thread stitch used to finish the edge of one layer during the construction process.

Serge-gather—Several serger techniques are possible for gathering an edge. You can use the differential feed on the 2.0 setting. Another option is to tighten your needle tension and lengthen your stitch. Or simply serge over heavy thread with a balanced stitch, being careful not to catch the heavy thread in the serging. Then, after anchoring one end, pull the heavy thread to gather the edge to any specific length. A fourth option is to loosen the needle tension, serge, and then pull up the needle thread.

Serge-seam—Most often a wide, standard N-length, and balanced 3- or 3/4-thread stitch used to seam two layers together.

Short stitch—A .75mm to 2mm serged stitch length.

Standard N length—The middle stitch-length setting on a *Hobbylock,* equal to about 3mm.

Standard N width—The middle stitch-width setting on a *Hobbylock,* equal to about 3.5mm.

Stitch-in-the-ditch—Stitching directly on top of a previous seamline to secure another layer positioned on the underside. Often used for nearly invisible stitching when applying a binding to an edge.

Straight-stitch—A medium-length (10-12 stitches/inch) straight stitch on a conventional sewing machine.

Thread chain—The joined loops formed by serging on a properly threaded machine with no fabric.

Top-stitch—A conventional-machine straight-stitch (10-12 stitches/inch) used to attach one layer (often serge-finished) to another. Top-stitching also can be used as a decorative design detail.

Wide stitch—A 5mm to 7.5mm serged stitch width.

Woolly nylon—One of our favorite decorative threads that became popular with the advent of serger sewing. A crimped nylon thread, it fluffs out to fill in any see-through spaces on a decorative edge.

Zigzag stitch—A basic stitch on a conventional sewing machine that forms a back-and-forth pattern similar to herringbone.

Mail-Order Resources

We recommend that every serger enthusiast develop a special relationship with his or her local dealers and retailers for convenient advice and inspiration, plus the ease of coordinating purchases. However, when specialty items cannot be found locally, or when a home-sewer lives several miles from a sewing retailer, mail-order specialists are a worthwhile option.

The following list will make your search for these resources a breeze. Our list is for reference only and does not carry our endorsement or guarantee. (We have not knowingly included any questionable items or firms.)

 Special Tip: To streamline information gathering, be specific even when simply requesting samples or specific product brochures. Let the company know exactly what you are looking for, such as color, fiber, texture, or size.

 Authors' note: In today's volatile business climate, any mail-order source list will change frequently. Please send your comments on any out-of-business notifications or unsatisfactory service to *Update Newsletters,* 2269 Chestnut #269, San Francisco, CA 94123.

Key to Abbreviations and Symbols:

SASE= self-addressed, stamped (first-class) envelope

L-SASE = large SASE (2-oz. first-class postage)

* = refundable with order

= for information, brochure or catalog

 Note: Check with your postmaster regarding Canadian mail.

Serger Company

Pfaff American Sales Corp.
610 Winters Ave.
Paramus, NJ 07653
(manufacturer of *Hobbylock* sergers)

Great Serger Notions

Aardvark Adventures, P.O. Box 2449, Livermore, CA 94551, 415/443-2687. Books, beads, buttons, bangles, plus an unusual assortment of related products. Decorative serging thread, including metallics. $1#.

The Bee Lee Company, P.O. Box 36108-B, Dallas, TX 75235. Complete selection of threads, zippers, notions, and trims, including western styles. Free#.

Catherine's, Rt. 6, Box 1227, Lexington, NC 27292, 704/798-1595. Serger threads and more at wholesale prices. Minimum order $35. School quantity discounts. $2 and L-SASE for thread color card.

Clotilde, Inc., 1909 SW First Ave., Ft. Lauderdale, FL 33315, 305/761-8655. Catalog of over 1,200 items, including special serger threads and notions, the *Perfect Pleater* and other sewing tools and supplies, and books and videos. $1#.

Custom Zips, P.O. Box 1200, South Norwalk, CT 06856. Zippers cut to order. $2#.

The Cutting Edge, P.O. Box 397, St. Peters, MO 63376. Serger notions, including coned threads (all-purpose and decorative), needle threaders, patterns, and carrying cases. $1#.

D & E Distributing, 199 N. El Camino Real #F-242, Encinitas, CA 92024. Decorative threads and yarns, including silk, rayon, and Madeira metallics. L-SASE#.

The Embroidery Stop, 1042 Victory Dr., Yardley, PA 19067. Threads, yarns, and needles. $1#.

Fit For You, 781 Golden Prados Dr., Diamond Bar, CA 91795, 714/861-5021. Sewing notions, serger accessories, videos, and square-dance patterns. L-SASE#.

Home-Sew, Dept. S, Bethlehem, PA 18018. Basic notions, trims, coned serger threads, and tools. Free#.

Jacquart's, 505 E. McLeod, Ironwood, MI 49938, 906/932-1339. Zippers. $1#.

Maryland Trims, P.O. Box 3508, Silver Spring, MD 20901. Laces, sewing notions, and supplies. $1.75#.

Mill End Store, Box 02098, Portland, OR 97202, 503/236-1234. Broad selection of notions, trims, serger threads, and accessories. SASE#.

Nancy's Notions, Ltd., P.O. Box 683, Beaver Dam, WI 53916, 414/887-0391. Over 300 sewing notions and accessories, serger threads and tools, interfacings and fabrics, and books and videos. Free#.

National Thread & Supply, 695 Red Oak Rd., Stockbridge, GA 30281, 800/847-1001, ext. 1688; in GA, 404/389-9115. Name-brand sewing supplies and notions. Free#.

Newark Dressmaker Supply, P.O. Box 2448, Lehigh Valley, PA 18001, 215/837-7500. Sewing notions, trims, buttons, decorative threads, and serger supplies. Free#.

The Perfect Notion, 566 Hoyt St., Darien, CT 06820, 203/968-1257. Hard-to-find notions and serger threads (including its exclusive *ThreadFuse* melt adhesive thread). $1#.

Serge and Sew Notions, 11761 99th Ave. N., Maple Grove, MN 55369, 612/493-2449. Serger threads, books, patterns, furniture, fabrics, and more, priced 20-40% below retail. $2.50*#. Swatch club, $6 for six months.

Serging Ahead, P.O. Box 45, Grandview, MO 64030. Serger threads, books, and patterns. $1#.

Sew-Art International, P.O. Box 550, Bountiful, UT 84010. Decorative threads, notions, and accessories. Free#.

Sew Craft, P.O. Box 1869, Warsaw, IN 46580, 219/269-4046. Books, decorative threads, and notions.

Sew/Fit Co., P.O. Box 565, La Grange, IL 60525, 312/579-3222. Sewing notions and accessories; modular tables for serger/sewing machine setup; books. Free#.

Sewing Emporium, 1087 Third Ave., Chula Vista, CA 92010, 619/420-3490. Hard-to-find sewing notions, sewing machine and serger cabinets and accessories, and serger threads and accessories. $2#.

The Sewing Place, 100 West Rincon Ave., Suite 105, Campbell, CA 95008. Sewing machine and serger needles and feet, plus books by Gale Grigg Hazen. Specify your brand and model if ordering machine accessories. L-SASE#.

The Sewing Workshop, 2010 Balboa St., San Francisco, CA 94121, 415/221-SEWS. Unique designer notions. L-SASE#.

Solo Slide Fasteners, Inc., P.O. Box 528, Stoughton, MA 02072, 800/343-9670. All types and lengths of zippers; other selected notions. Free#.

Speed Stitch, 3113-D Broadpoint Dr., Harbor Heights, FL 33983, 800/874-4115. Machine-art kits and supplies, including all-purpose, decorative, and specialty serging threads, books, and accessories. $3*#.

Thread Discount & Sales, 7105 S. Eastern, Bell Gardens, CA 90201, 213/562-3438. Coned polyester thread. SASE#.

Threads & Things, P.O. Box 83190, San Diego, CA 92138, 619/440-8760. 100% rayon thread. Free#.

Threads West, 422 E. State St., Redlands, CA 92373, 714/793-4405 or 0214. Coned thread, serger parts, and accessories. SASE for free thread color list.

Treadleart, 25834 Narbonne Ave., Suite I, Lomita, CA 90717, 800/327-4222. Books, serging supplies, notions, decorative threads, and creative inspiration. $1.50#.

T-Rific Products Co., P.O. Box 911, Winchester, OR 97495. Coned serger thread. Thread color chart, $1.25.

Two Brothers, 1602 Locust St., St. Louis, MO 63103. Zipper assortment. SASE#.

YLI Corporation, 482 N. Freedom Blvd., Provo, UT 84601, 800/854-1932 or 801/377-3900. Decorative, specialty, serger, and all-purpose threads, yarns, and ribbons. $1.50#.

Other Publications by the Authors

Serger Update Newsletter, P.O. Box 5026, Harlan IA 51537. The only periodical devoted entirely to serging news and techniques. Published monthly ($39 annual subscription).

Distinctive Serger Gifts & Crafts, Chilton Book Company, 1989. The first book with one-of-a-kind serger projects using ingenious methods and upscale ideas, by Naomi Baker and Tammy Young.

Innovative Serging, Chilton Book Company, 1989. State-of-the-art techniques for overlock sewing, by Gail Brown and Tammy Young.

Innovative Sewing, Chilton Book Company, 1990. The newest, best, and fastest sewing techniques, by Gail Brown and Tammy Young.

Know Your baby lock, Chilton Book Company, 1990. Ornamental serging techniques for all *baby lock* serger models, by Naomi Baker and Tammy Young.

Know Your White Superlock, Chilton Book Company, 1991. Ornamental serging techniques for all *Superlock* serger models, by Naomi Baker and Tammy Young.

Simply Serge Any Fabric, Chilton Book Company, 1990. Tips and techniques for successfully serging all types of fabric, by Naomi Baker and Tammy Young.

Index

Accessories, *Hobbylock,* 10-12
All-purpose thread, 27
Appliqué, serged, 161-165
Appliquéd Evening Bag, 162-165

Balanced decorative edges
  picot-braid, 52
  project for, 53-54
  serge-corded, 50-51
  serge-corded variations, 52
  serge-scalloped, 49-50
  use of, 49
Balanced flatlocking, 121-122
Basic seams
  decorative, 33
  decorative French, 36
  hidden lapped serging
    technique, 34-35
  lapped, 36
  mock flat-felled, 36-37
  project for, 37-38
  reversed decorative, 35-36
  serging, 33
Batting, 29
Bead-edged Flower, 132-133
Beaded piping, 131
Beading foot, 12, 51
Beads, 130-131
Bindings, decorative
  double-bound edge, 78-80
  double-bound seam, 41-42
  double-piped seam, 42-43
  double rolled-edge binding,
    93-96
  elasticized, 98-100
  serged, 86-89
  serged French, 39-41
  serged seam, 39
  serged self-binding, 75-78
  serge-piped, 89-93
Blanket stitch. *See*
    Reversible needle-wrap
    stitch

Blindhem foot, 11
"Bonding", 1-2
Braided trim, 98
Braids
  puffed serged, 103-106
  quick-fused self-braid,
    73-75
  serged couching, 109-110
  serged-fold self-braid,
    70-73
  serged picot, 106-109
  tear-away, 101-103
Buttonholes
  serge-bound, 149-152
  serged elastic buttonloops
    152-154

Canvas Tote Bag, 76-78
Chain art. *See* Serger chain art
Chain-loop serging, 169-170
Christmas Tree Bags, 59-60
Closures. *See* Serged closures
Constructing fabric, 168
Corded flatlocking, 120-121
Cording, 157
Couched Tree Ornament, 35
Cutwork Tablecloth, 167-168

Decorative bindings. *See*
    Bindings
Decorative edges. *See* Edges
Decorative flatlocking, 120-124
Decorative French seam, 36
Decorative seams. *See* Seams
Decorative serged closures.
    See Serged closures
Decorative serging techniques.
    See Serging techniques
Decorative threads. *See* Threads
Decorative trims. *See* Trims
Differential-feed gathering, 112
Double-bound edge, 78-80
Double-bound seam, 41-42
Double-Bow Pillow, 37-38
Double chainstitch shirring, 115
Double-picot braid, 107
Double-piped seam, 42-43
Double rolled edge, 57

Double rolled-edge binding, 93-96
Double rolled-edge braid, 93,
    94-96
Double-stretch trim, 97
Double-wrapped Tassel, 159-160
Dressed-up Cosmetic Bag,
    142-144

Edges, decorative
  balanced
    picot-braid, 52
    project for, 53-54
    serge-corded, 50-51
    serge-corded
      variations,52
    serge-scalloped, 49-50
    use of, 49
  fishline ruffles, 61-63
  reversible-edge binding
    stitch, 66-67
  reversible needle-wrap
    stitch, 67-69
  rolled
    double, 57
    lettucing, 56-57
    picot, 58
    project for, 59-60
    scalloped, 58
    serge-o-fold, 58
    technique of, 55-56
    tuck-and-roll, 59
    use of, 54
  wire-shaped, 63-65
Elastic foot, 11
Elasticized binding, 98-100
Elasticized mock piping, 83-84
Elasticized piping, 81-82
Elasticized trims, 96-98, 100-101
Elastic thread, 28
Embellished Chiffon Scarf, 171
Embellished fabric, 168-171
Embellished zipper tape,
    139-140

Fabrics
    constructing, 168
    embellished, 168-171
    ornamenting, 169-171
    serging, 3
Feet, *Hobbylock,* 10-12
Fiberfill, 29
Filler-cord gathering, 112-113
Fine wire, 29
Fishline, 29
Fishline ruffles, 61-63, 118
5-thread safety stitch, 5
Flatlocked fringe, 124-125
Flatlocked patches, 170
Flatlocked seams
    balanced, 121-122
    corded, 120-121
    decorative, 120-124
    over lace, 128
    perfecting, 44-45
    project for, 46-47
    reinforcing, 45-46
    over ribbon, 128
    safety-stitch, 121
    serging, 44
    over yarn, 129
Flatlocking. *See* Flatlocked
    seams
Fringed Triangle Scarf,
    126-127
Fringing, 124-127, 157-158
Frog Closures, 105-106
Fusible thread, 28

Gathering, 111-113

Heart-shaped Jewelry Holder,
    129-130
Hidden lapped serging
    technique, 34-35
Hobbylock
    accessories, 10-12
    bonding with, 1-2
    company, 175
    creativity and, 30-31
    features of, 5, 6-7
    feet, 10-12
    history, 172

lessons and, using 4-5
loopers of, 3, 22
mail-order resources for,
    175-177
maintenance of, 13-15
notions for, 175-177
serging strategies with, 3-4
sewing machine and, 1, 3-4
sewing strategies with, 3-4
stitch formation and, 5,
    8-10
Hobo Bag, 43-44

Lace, 116-120, 128
Lace-edge Handkerchief, 72-73
Lace-trimmed wires, 118-119
Lacy fishline ruffles, 118
Lapped placket, 137-138
Lapped zippers, 136-141
Lapped seam, 36
Lettucing, 56-57
Loopers, 3, 22

Mail-order resources, 175-177
Maintenance, 13-15
Mock flat-felled seam, 36-37
Mock hemstitching, 122
Mock piping, 82-83
Monofilament nylon thread, 28
Monogrammed Hand Towel,
    110

Narrow rolled-edge foot, 11

Ornamenting fabric, 169-171
Overlock stitches, 9

Padded Picture Frame, 90-93
Patches, flatlocked, 170
Pearls, 130-131
Picot-braid edge, 52
Picot-braid variations, 107
Picot rolled edge, 58
Picot-trimmed Hat, 108-109
Piping
    beaded, 131
    elasticized, 81-82
    elasticized mock, 83-84
    mock, 82-83
    serged, 84-86

Pressing, 27
Pretty Pencil Cup, 102-103
Projects
    Appliquéd Evening Bag,
      162-165
    Bead-edged Flower, 132-133
    Canvas Tote Bag, 76-78
    Christmas Tree Bags, 59-60
    Couched Tree Ornament,
      135
    Cutwork Tablecloth, 167-168
    Double-Bow Pillow, 37-38
    Double-wrapped Tassel,
      159-160
    Dressed-up Cosmetic Bag,
      142-144
    Embellished Chiffon Scarf,
      171
    Fringed Triangle Scarf,
      126-127
    Frog Closures, 105-106
    Heart-shaped Jewelry
      Holder, 129-130
    Hobo Bag, 43-44
    Lace-edged Handkerchief,
      72-73
    Monogrammed Hand
      Towel, 110
    Padded Picture Frame, 90-93
    Picot-trimmed Hat, 108-109
    Pretty Pencil Cup, 102-103
    Quickie Shoe Bags, 74-75
    Quick Potholder, 68-69
    Quick Slip, 46-47
    Ruffled Doily, 62-63
    Ruffled Jar Cover, 100-101
    Sampler Pin Cushion, 123-
      124
    Serge-bound Table Runner,
      87-89
    Serged Pencil Case, 140-141
    Serge-finished Collar, 153-
      154
    Serge-piped Book Cover, 84-
      86
    Serger-Lace Flower, 119-120
    Shirred Ponytail Tube, 115-
      116

Show-off Pillow, 79-80
Sunburst T-shirt, 53-54
Tailored Garment Bag, 147-149
Three-Button Belt, 151-152
Tooth Fairy Pillow, 94-96
Wind Twister, 64-65
Wool Lap Robe, 66-67
Publications, serging, 178
Puffed serged braid, 103-106

Quick-fused self-braid, 73-75
Quickie Shoe Bags, 74-75
Quick Potholder, 68-69
Quick Slip, 46-47

Reinforced flatlock seaming, 45-46
Reversed decorative seam, 35-36
Reversed decorative seam zipper, 138-139
Reversible-edge binding stitch, 66-67
Reversible needle-wrap stitch, 67-69
Ribbon, 128
Ribbon foot, 12
Rolled edges
    double, 57
    lettucing, 56-57
    picot, 58
    project for, 59-60
    scalloped, 58
    serge-o-fold, 58
    technique of, 55-56
    tuck-and-roll, 59
    use of, 54
Ruffled Doily, 62-63
Ruffled Jar Cover, 100-101

Safety-stitch flatlocking, 121
Sample book, 30
Sampler Pin Cushion, 123-124
Scalloped rolled edge, 58

Seams, decorative
    basic
        decorative, 33
        decorative French, 36
        hidden-lapped serging technique, 34-35
        lapped, 36
        mock flat-felled, 36-37
        project for, 37-38
        reversed, 35-36
    flatlocked
        perfecting, 44-45
        project for, 46-47
        reinforcing, 45-46
        serging, 44
    serge-bound
        double-bound, 41-42
        double-piped, 42-43
        project for, 43-44
        serged French binding, 39-41
        serged seam binding, 39
        serging, 38
    serging, 32
Seam sealant, 32-33
Sequins, 131-132
Serge-a-fold, 58
Serge-bound buttonholes, 149-152
Serge-bound seams
    double-bound, 41-42
    double-piped, 42-43
    project for, 43-44
    serged French binding, 39-41
    serged seam binding, 39
    serging, 38
Serge-bound Table Runner, 87-89
Serge-corded edge, 50-51
Serge-corded variations, 52
Serge-couching, 133-135
Serged appliqué, 161-165
Serged binding, 86-89
Serged closures
    lapped zippers, 136-141
    serge-bound buttonholes, 149-152
    serged elastic button loops, 152-154

serge-picked zippers, 144-149
    top-stitched zippers, 136-141
    zipped double-bound edge, 141-144
Serged couching braid, 109-110
Serged elastic button loops, 152-154
Serged-fold self-braid, 70-73
Serged French binding, 39-41
Serged Pencil Case, 140-141
Serged picot braid, 106-109
Serged piping
    elasticized, 81-82
    elasticized mock, 83-84
    mock, 82-83
    project for, 84-86
    technique of, 80-81
Serged seam binding, 39
Serged self-binding, 75-78
Serge-fagoting, 122-123
Serge-finished Collar, 153-154
Serge-fold self-braid, 70-73
Serge-picked zippers, 144-149
Serge-piped binding, 89-93
Serge-piped Book Cover, 84-86
Serger. See Hobbylock
Serger applications
    embellished fabric, 168-171
    serged appliqué, 161-165
    serger chain art, 155-160
    serger cutwork, 165-168
Serger chain art
    project for, 159-160
    thread-chain cording, 157
    thread-chain fringe, 157-158
    thread-chain tassel, 158-159
    use of, 155-157
Serger cutwork, 165-168
Serger lace, 116-120
Serger-Lace Flower, 119-120
Serger lace tucks, 118
Serger notions, 175-177
Serger thread, 27
Serge-scalloped edge, 49-50
Serge-shirring, 113-115

Serging. *See also* Serging
    techniques
    basic seams, 33
    chain-loop, 169-170
    decorative seams, 32
    decorative threads, 22-24
    decorative threads and, 19,
        22-27
    fabric, 3
    flatlocked seams, 44
    other threads and, 27-28
    publications, 178
    sample book, 30
    serge-bound seam, 38
    shaping materials and, 28-29
    supplies, 29
    tension and, 16-19
    terms, 172-174
    over trims, 127-130
Serging techniques, decorative
    decorative flatlocking,
        120-124
    fringing, 124-127
    gathering, 111-113
    hidden lapped, 34-35
    sequin, bead, and pearl
        application, 130-133
    serge-couching, 133-135
    serger lace, 116-120
    serging over trim, 127-130
    hand sewing strategies, 3-4
    shirring, 113-116
Sewing machine, 1, 3-4
Sewing strategies, 3-4. *See
    also* Serging strategies
Shaping materials, 28-29
Shirred Ponytail Tube,
    115-116
Shirring, 113-116
Show-off Pillow, 79-80
Single-picot braid, 106-107
Single-stretch trim, 96-97
Stabilized lace, 117-118
Standard *Hobbylock*
    accessories, 12
Stitches. *See also* Seams
    5-thread safety, 5
    overlock, 9

3-thread overlock, 9
3/4-thread overlock, 9
2-thread double chainstitch,
    10
    uneven, 26
Stretch picot braid, 107-108
Stretch-trim variations, 97-98
Sunburst T-shirt, 53-54
Supplies
    mail-order sources for, 175-
        177
    serger, 29-30

Tailored Garment Bag, 147-149
Tassels, 158-160
Tear-away braid, 101-103
Tension
    adjusting, 17
    balancing, 17-19
    gathering, 111-112
    importance of, 16
    serging and, 16-19
    varying, 25
Thread-chain cording, 157
Thread-chain fringe, 157-158
Thread-chain gathering, 113
Thread-chain tassels, 158-159
Thread nets, 26
Threading tips, 24-27
Threads
    all-purpose, 27
    decorative
        combining, 27
        pressing, 27
        serging, 22-24
        sources for, 19, 22
        threading tips for, 24-27
    elastic, 28
    fusible, 28
    monafilament nylon, 28
3-thread overlock stitch, 9, 44
Three-Button Belt, 151-152
3/4-thread overlock stitch, 9
Tooth Fairy Pillow, 94-96
Top-stitched placket, 137-138
Top-stitched zippers, 136-141
Trims, decorative
    braided, 98
    double rolled-edge braid,
        93-96

elasticized, 96-98, 100-101
puffed serged braid, 103-106
quick-fused self-braid, 73-75
serged couching braid, 109-
    110
serged-fold self-braid, 70-73
serged picot braid, 106-109
serged piping
    elasticized, 81-82
    elasticized mock piping,
        83-84
    mock piping, 82-83
    project for, 84-86
    technique of, 80-81
serge-fold self-braid, 70-73
serging over, 127-130
tear-away braid, 101-103
Tuck-and-roll edge, 59
Tucked fringe, 125-126
Tucks, 118
2-thread double chainstitch,
    10

Wind Twister, 64-65
Wire-shaped edges, 63, 65
Wool Lap Robe, 66-67
Workpiece guide plate, 12

Yarn, 129

Zipped double-bound edge,
    141-144
Zippers
    basic lapped and
        topstitched, 136-137
    embellished zipper tape,
        139-140
    lapped and top-stitched
        placket, 137-138
    project for, 140-141
    reversed decorative seam,
        138-139
    serged-picked, 144-149
    zipped double-bound edge,
        141-144